Southern Living®
Cookbook
Library

The
Casseroles
Cookbook

Copyright © 1971 Oxmoor House, Inc.
All rights reserved.
Library of Congress Catalog Number: 76-56598
ISBN: 0-8487-0346-4

Cover: Herbed Beef Rolls (page 28)
Left: Osso Buco (page 36)

contents

preface

The tantalizing aroma of meats and vegetables blending their flavors . . . the mouth-watering sight of a bubbling-hot meal-in-a-dish . . . the sheer joy of popping your entire supper into the oven to bake . . . welcome to the wonderful world of casseroles!

It *is* a wonderful world, for casseroles are among the most versatile meals known. *Southern Living* homemakers know how wonderful casseroles are — and they have invented equally wonderful recipes. Just look through these pages. Beef and veal . . . ground beef . . . pork . . . poultry . . . fish and shellfish . . . lamb and game . . . combination meats . . . vegetables . . . cereals, pasta, egg, and cheese . . . recipes for all these delicious casseroles abound throughout this colorful new book.

And there's more! This book about casseroles tells you all about the fine art of casserole cookery. About the many types of casserole dishes and how to choose the right one for your recipe. About how to freeze ready-to-eat casseroles. About how to use herbs and spices to bring out the full, rich flavor of casserole cookery.

This is a book for you, today's homemaker, from the kitchens of cooks throughout the Southland. This is a book you will come to depend on for truly memorable casserole dishes. Welcome to the wonderful world of casserole cookery — southern style!

Seasonings add marvelous flavor to casseroles — and bring out the full, natural flavor of every ingredient. There are three types of seasonings — herbs, spices, and natural vegetable seasonings. Herbs can be found fresh, dried, or powdered. Fresh spices are available whole, or you can add them to your spice rack in powdered form. Vegetable seasonings are usually fresh, although some are sold in salt form as well.

HERBS

Herbs come from plants that do not have woody tissue; consequently, they die immediately after flowering. Freshly picked herbs have the best flavor for cooking. Dried herbs are four times more powerful than fresh ones; therefore, less than a teaspoon of dried herbs will equal a tablespoon of

herbs & spices
FOR CASSEROLES

fresh. Powdered herbs are twice as powerful as dried ones. Dried and powdered herbs should be stored in a cool, dark place as their flavor will change if they are exposed to heat or sunlight.

Which herbs do you use? If you are just beginning to experiment with herbs, we suggest that you start with the so-called "basic" herbs, those most commonly used. After you have mastered the art of using these, try your hand at herb combinations and the more unusual herbs.

Basil is a delicate and fragrant herb especially popular in tomato dishes or in those with a tomato sauce base. Its rich flavor is a nice addition to beef, veal, pork, lamb, and seafood casseroles. Try basil with vegetables, too, especially peas, string beans, potatoes, and spinach.

Chive has often been described as "toned-down onion." It tastes best when fresh. Its piquant flavor combines delightfully with beef, lamb, veal, and poultry casseroles.

Dill has a much stronger flavor than either basil or chive. It should be added near the end of cooking and is particularly good in fish and beef dishes. Use with a very light touch.

Sweet marjoram is a wonderfully versatile herb. It can be used to good advantage in all meat, fish and seafood casseroles, and in such vegetable dishes as peas, spinach, and green beans.

Rosemary is one of the most fragrant of all herbs. It adds a mild flavor to game, beef, lamb, pork, veal, and fish casseroles. And it is excellent with vegetable dishes — cauliflower, peas, and spinach.

Thyme is always used in an herb bouquet with bay leaf. It adds an interesting flavor to beans and potatoes as well as seafood and fish casseroles. And it goes well with beef, game, lamb, veal, and pork. It is indispensable in Creole dishes. Use sparingly.

Oregano has enjoyed renewed popularity in the United States, thanks in part to the enthusiasm for Italian cookery. It is often used with tomato-based dishes in combination with basil.

Parsley is a mild-flavored herb as important for garnishing as it is for seasoning. It goes well with all meat dishes. Or try mixing it with buttered crumbs as a casserole topping. And here's an extra bonus: parsley is an excellent source of iron.

Sage has a powerful flavor and should be used with a very light touch. It is a vital ingredient in stuffings and is particularly good with mild-flavored meat dishes, such as those made with pork, veal, or poultry.

Mint is one of the most popular herbs. Add dried mint leaves to cooked foods shortly before cooking time is up. It is excellent in most lamb dishes and brings an exciting flavor note to peas, carrots, and snap beans.

Bay leaf is used in herb bouquets with thyme. It is cooked for a short time with the dish and is removed before serving. It has a bitter taste if eaten. Bay leaf brings a tempting flavor to hearty meat casseroles, especially those made of beef.

To these eleven basic herbs, add others as you progress. Certainly you'll want to include *savory,* which adds interesting flavor to peas and bean casseroles.

Tarragon is an ancient favorite highly prized for its flavorful contribution to poultry and veal casserole dishes. And don't forget *garlic.* This much maligned herb is one of the most important in French and Italian cuisines. It must be used with a light touch, but brings unusual flavor to otherwise ordinary casseroles. For example, try rubbing the inside of your casserole dish with a cut clove of garlic. The hint of exotic flavor will delight your guests' palates.

SPICES

Herbs are not the only seasonings to bring flavor notes to your casseroles. Spices are plant seeds or are prepared by grinding or chopping plant roots, nuts, fruits, or bark.

Some of the basic spices are listed below with a description of how they might be used to add new life to your casserole cookery.

Caraway, a seed most often used in bread and cake making, is also a flavorful addition to beef casseroles or those made with potatoes or cabbage.

Cayenne is ground from the seeds and pods of various peppers. This spice should be used with a very light touch. It accents the natural flavors of savory dishes – those with spicy sauces or those made from meats which have been marinated. Try it with a meat pie for a real flavor treat.

Curry powder is a combination of eight or ten spices ground together. It has a very sharp flavor and is used most often in Indian cooking. If you want to experiment, try it with poultry, seafood, fish casseroles, or those made with vegetables or rice. One warning: curry powder scorches and changes flavor when cooked at high temperature. Keep the temperature as low as possible.

Paprika, the ground powder of the pepper plant, is a favorite mild-flavored spice. It adds color to pale meat dishes and to fish casseroles. Its mild flavor highlights casseroles made of fish, poultry, pork, or veal.

Allspice is most often used in combination with other spices in fruit dishes and desserts. But try just a touch of it in your next beef casserole or meat pie. You'll be delighted with the results!

VEGETABLE SEASONINGS

Seasonings do not have to be limited to the usual herbs and spices. For thousands of years, cooks have used vegetables for their seasoning value. Foremost among the seasoning vegetables are the various *onions.* Scallions add a piquant flavor to sauces. Onions, used in moderation, are a delicious flavor note in almost every casserole.

Try a few *mushrooms* in your next casserole – they have a distinct flavor which perks up every dish.

And *celery* is a real bonus! Chop a few celery stalks and add them to your next tomato-based dish. Add chopped leaves to cauliflower, cheese, or game dishes. Your family will applaud!

Many of the seasonings mentioned here are available in a salt form. The presence of salt base may change the flavor of any seasoning and make it rancid. Use seasoning salts with care, and taste as you go.

One word of caution. If the casserole you are making is destined for the freezer before serving, use a very light touch with your seasonings. Many herbs and spices will change flavor during the freezing process. Some herbs – such as chive – become soggy if they are frozen and thawed. It is a better idea to season lightly, freeze, then taste the dish when it is reheated and season to suit your palate.

As you become accustomed to experimenting with herbs and spices, you and your family will begin to discover great flavor treats awaiting you. A skillful touch of seasoning turns a casserole of leftovers into a family-pleasing treat. Try it for yourself and see!

One of the joys of casserole cookery lies in the prepare-ahead feature of these one-dish meals. Nearly every kind of casserole can be prepared ahead of time and frozen. Then on that hectic and busy day, just take out the frozen dish and pop it into a preheated oven. While you sit and unwind, your supper is cooking!

The key to successful freezing lies in knowing (1) how well the various ingredients in your casserole will freeze and (2) what steps you must take to ensure that a frozen casserole tastes and looks no different from its freshly prepared counterpart.

INGREDIENTS

Different foods react to freezing in different ways. Some flavors or textures

freezing instructions
FOR CASSEROLES

may change during the freezing process — certain of these changes may spell disaster for your casserole.

Eggs: Hard-cooked egg whites become tough when they are frozen unless they are first put through a sieve. Egg yolks should be diced or sieved before freezing.

Sauces and mayonnaise sometimes separate during freezing. In most instances, their original consistency can be restored by stirring during the thawing process. Sauces with cheese and milk tend to curdle if they are frozen and reheated. And thickened sauces will probably need thinning down. Avoid freezing sauces which are egg-based.

Cheese does not freeze well. If your casserole recipe calls for a topping of grated or sliced cheese, add it when you are ready to thaw and serve the dish.

Seasonings change considerably during freezing. Some, such as parsley and chive, may become soggy after thawing. Others change flavor: onion and salt are considerably diminished in flavor as are most herb seasonings. Garlic and clove become unpleasantly strong. Curry develops a musty flavor. The best rule of thumb is to avoid seasoning casseroles to be frozen until you are ready to serve them.

Potatoes should seldom be frozen and never if they have been cut into small pieces — they break down when thawed and become mushy. Potatoes should be added to a casserole when it is being thawed.

Noodles, spaghetti, and macaroni all have a better flavor if they are added during the thawing process.

Fats become rancid after about two months of freezing time. Sauces made with high proportions of fat may not freeze well.

Meats which have been frozen may be thawed, cooked in a casserole, and then refrozen with the rest of the dish without affecting the flavor of the meat. However, very small pieces of meat may dry out if they are frozen.

PREPARING CASSEROLES FOR THE FREEZER

Because the thawing process involves cooking, casseroles to be frozen should not be completely cooked before they are frozen. If you plan to freeze your casserole, remove it from the stove or oven and chill as quickly as possible, either in the refrigerator or by setting the casserole over a pan of ice water.

Casseroles may be frozen in their dish or in a specially prepared cooking "package." This do-it-yourself cooking "package" will cut down on the number of dishes you'll need. Line an empty casserole dish with aluminum foil, allowing a generous overlap on all sides. Then pour the casserole ingredients into the lined dish, bake – if that is required by your recipe – and chill according to the directions above. Freeze as quickly as possible. When your casserole is solidly frozen, lift out the aluminum foil "dish" with the casserole mixture and wrap according to the directions below.

Wrapping is critically important to successful freezing. Nothing can dry frozen food faster than air in the package. Air left in packaged food draws on the moisture and juices of that food to form a frost. That frost, of course, gives off the odors of the food. The result may be a mixture of flavors among your frozen foods and a radically different taste from the one originally present.

To overcome this problem moisture-proof, vapor-proof wrappings are a must. If you are using pre-formed packages, their size should be scaled the size of the casserole being frozen. With today's modern packaging industry, there is an entire world of wrapping available for you.

If you want to store several casseroles at once, consider the merits of the pint, quart, and two-quart size containers especially made for freezing. They are especially designed to allow you to maximize your freezer space. If you do use pre-formed casserole packages, be sure to allow 1 1/2 inch head space for expansion during freezing.

Many homemakers prefer do-it-yourself packages. Casseroles may be frozen in their dish, then wrapped. The commonly used wrapping papers are aluminum foil or special laminated papers. Almost all such packages require special sealing with either freezer tape or a sealing iron.

To wrap a frozen casserole in paper, use the lock-seal method. Place the casserole in the center of a large piece of paper. Bring the ends together and fold them into an interlocking seam. Fold the paper down tightly against your casserole. Reverse the package so that the seam is against your working surface. Turn the package so that one of the open ends is near your body and the other one faces away from you. Pleat fold the end nearest you, and fold it over again before pressing it against the package. Hold the folded end tightly against you and gradually force air out of the open end of the package. Fold the remaining open end.

All packages destined for the freezer should be labeled with the name of the casserole and the date of freezing. If you save casserole dishes by using foil liners, you may want to note in which dish your foil liner was molded. With this information, all you have to do is pop the casserole into its original dish when you are ready to thaw and serve.

The freezing process described above is recommended for home freezers. The temperature in these freezers is usually zero degrees or lower, and the freezing takes place rapidly. The same results will not necessarily come about if you use the freezing compartment of your refrigerator, which is usually at a warmer temperature. Avoid using your refrigerator's freezer for long-term freezing, unless you can bring its temperature down to at least zero.

FREEZING

The freezing process should be completed as quickly as possible. Food will freeze more rapidly if it is placed near or touching the freezing surfaces — the walls of your freezer. Never overload your freezer by putting several packages of unfrozen food into it at once. Try to leave plenty of room for the frozen air to circulate around your packages of frozen food.

Most casseroles can be safely frozen for three to four months. Some may even last six months — the reason for the differing lengths of time is the ingredients used. Many vegetable casseroles will be delicious as long as six months after freezing. Casseroles with a high concentration of fat in the sauce should be used within two months.

THAWING

Casseroles may be thawed in the refrigerator and then heated thoroughly before serving. However, a quicker method is to heat the frozen dish in the oven, at the cooking temperature called for in the original recipe. Should you use the freezer-to-oven method of thawing, be sure to allow longer than the original cooking time. Even though most casseroles are almost cooked when they are frozen, these directions should still be followed. This method works well with all but very large casseroles. Thawing them in the oven may produce singed edges and a still-frozen center. If you are preparing such a large recipe, it is better to plan to thaw it in the refrigerator, then heat it thoroughly in the oven just prior to serving.

Nearly all of today's modern casserole dishes go from freezer to oven with perfect aplomb. However, glass ovenware must be placed in a preheated oven. With the wide variety of dishes on the market, you are certain to find just what you need. And to help you, we have assembled information on the various kinds of dishes in the next section.

To American homemakers, a casserole is a one-dish main course or even a complete meal in a dish. But to their French counterparts, a casserole is the special kind of dish for oven or top-of-the-stove cooking in which these meals are prepared. These dishes come in many sizes, shapes, and materials.

Covered baking dishes may be round, oblong, or square. Most have handles. They are available in 1, 1 1/2, and 2-quart sizes.

Shallow rectangular baking dishes are either rectangular, as their name implies, or oval in shape. Some of the larger sizes are divided so that two casseroles may be baked at once. The most common sizes are the 1 1/2-quart – 10 x 6 x 1 1/2; the 2-quart – 11 1/2 x 7 1/2 x 1 1/2; and the 3-quart – 13 x 9 x 2.

Shallow round open baking pans are excellent values because they double as

types of dishes

cake pans. They are recommended if you bake many egg or au gratin dishes.

Individual casseroles are available in either earthenware or one of the other oven-proof materials. The usual size for an individual serving is one cup. A recipe for one quart casserole will fill four individual dishes.

Nice-to-have dishes include souffle dishes which are straight-sided and reserved for souffles only, and ramekins, a kind of individual souffle dish also good for making special egg casseroles.

What are today's casserole dishes made of? Just about every material from the earthenware used in the French and Swiss casseroles to the freezer-to-oven glassware so popular with American homemakers. One of the most popular – and best – materials is enamel-covered cast iron. It is sturdy, colorful, and will keep food warm for hours after baking. There are oven-proof glass casseroles of the Pyrex type. If you want to dress up these dishes, try draping them in brightly colored napkins, or setting them inside one of the new basket or metal casserole holders.

Earthenware dishes made of terra cotta are the oldest kind of casseroles and, some cooks profess, the very best. There are two major types of earthenware casseroles, the Swiss and the Parisian. Swiss casseroles have hollow handles which cool quickly after the dish is removed from heat, enabling the cook to handle the dish easily. Many Swiss casseroles have a pouring lip. They range in size from individual serving dishes to huge six quart ones. Paris casseroles are very similar to Swiss ones but have straighter sides.

Both Swiss and Parisian casseroles are made of medium thick earthenware and are beige on the outside and glazed brown on the inside and top. Many cooks say these casseroles can be used on top of the range as well as in the oven. However, it is recommended that you temper the earthenware with several oven bakings before using it on top of the stove. When used on the stove, be sure to protect the dish with an asbestos pad between it and the source of direct heat.

Bright and beautiful casserole dishes are available in California clay. Chip resistant and flameproof, these gaily colored casseroles are made from thick pottery glazed on the rims, the inside, and the cover. The body is unglazed, natural terra cotta. These warm earth colors bring lovely accents to your dinner table.

Finally, there are the tin-lined copper casserole dishes. These are the very finest dishes and, like all other fine things, they require special care. Copper is very soft and needs careful handling. A wooden spoon is a must for stirring, because wood will not scratch the delicate copper or its tin lining. The lining may wear out and need replacing. So although a joy to look at, copper casserole dishes may not be the most practical buy for a young and active family.

Whatever your preference, your new casserole dish should be conditioned before you use it. Fill it with lukewarm water and add a pinch of your favorite spices to the water. Place the dish in an oven set at low temperature for one hour. Turn the oven off and let the dish stay in it until the oven is cold. Pour out the water, and your dish is ready to use.

In addition to casserole dishes, there are many other pots and pans which are helpful to have for casserole preparation. A *double-boiler* is great for cheese sauces and egg dishes which must be cooked over gentle heat. The *single-pan chafing* dish and its deeper cousin, the *fondue pot,* are nice to have. They cook food over direct heat from alcohol, electric, or canned sources. *Bain-marie* (from the French word for water bath) *chafing dishes* combine the virtues of single-pan dishes with those of a double-boiler. This dish has two pans — one for cooking over direct heat, the other for cooking over water — and can also serve as a warmer for foods already cooked. This dish is an excellent investment that comes in a wide range of colors, materials, and sizes.

beef & veal

Beef and veal casseroles are all-time favorites with southern families. From the tomato-y rich goodness of Veal and Eggplant Casserole to the mushroom and onion flavor of California Casserole, beef and veal dishes are sure to bring compliments from family and guests alike.

This section contains the finest and favorite recipes southern homemakers have developed for beef and veal casseroles. In a hurry? Club Day Casserole is just what you need. This combination of stewing beef and mushrooms in its own rich sauce is topped with biscuits. Prepare it ahead of time, then just pop it into the oven — from oven to table in just a few short minutes.

When company is coming — or you just want to serve something deliciously different — try Rigatoni Special. It combines leftover beef, onions, garlic, tomatoes, and enchilada sauce in a hearty casserole.

And nothing could say "special" better than Venetian Veal. This Italian-style dish is easy to prepare and oh-so-good. The appetizing aroma of veal, celery, onion, carrots, and rich spices will have your family and guests more than ready to sit down and enjoy themselves.

These are just a few of the marvelous recipes you will find in the pages that follow. All are the home-tested favorites of southern homemakers, who now share them with you. They are sure to become your favorites, too.

CALIFORNIA CASSEROLE

2 lb. round steak	1/8 tsp. pepper
1/3 c. flour	1 can cream of mushroom soup
1 tsp. paprika	1 3/4 c. water
1/2 tsp. salt	1 3/4 c. cooked sm. onions

Cut the steak in 2-inch cubes. Mix the flour and paprika and dredge steak with flour mixture. Brown in small amount of hot fat in a skillet. Add the salt and pepper and place in a large casserole. Add the soup and water to drippings in skillet and bring to a boil, stirring constantly. Pour over steak and add the onions.

Dumplings

1 c. milk	2 c. flour
1/2 c. salad oil	1/2 tsp. salt
1 tsp. celery seed	1 tsp. onion flakes
1 tsp. poultry seasoning	1/3 c. melted margarine
4 tsp. baking powder	1 1/2 c. bread crumbs

Mix the milk and oil. Place the celery seed, poultry seasoning, baking powder, flour, salt and onion flakes in a large bowl and mix well. Add the milk mixture and stir until mixed. Drop by tablespoonfuls into margarine to coat, then roll in bread crumbs. Place on steak mixture. Bake at 425 degrees for 20 to 25 minutes. 8 servings.

Frances Dunbar, Ash Fork, Arizona

CASSEROLE INTERNATIONAL

3 c. cooked roast beef, cut in large cubes	1 c. tomato juice
	2 sm. cloves of garlic, minced

Buffet Casserole (page 17)

1/2 tsp. fines herbes
1 tsp. curry powder
1 tsp. minced green pepper
1 pkg. frozen chow mein
1 c. cooked fettucini

1/2 c. cooking sherry
1/2 c. grated sharp Cheddar
  cheese
2 tbsp. minced parsley

Place the roast beef, tomato juice, garlic, fines herbes, curry powder and green pepper in a saucepan and simmer for 15 minutes, adding tomato juice, if needed. Add the chow mein and simmer until thawed. Add fettucini and sherry and stir well. Place in a greased casserole and sprinkle with cheese and parsley. Bake in 300-degree oven for about 15 minutes.

Mrs. Harry Ransom, Austin, Texas

ELEGANT BEEF

1 clove of garlic, minced
1/2 c. chopped onion
2 tbsp. shortening
1/2 tsp. salt
1/8 tsp. pepper
1/4 c. flour
1 lb. sirloin, cut in 2-in.
  strips

1 3-oz. can sliced
  mushrooms
2 tbsp. catsup
1/2 to 1 c. beef bouillon
1/2 c. sour cream
Cooked wide noodles
Poppy seed to taste

Saute the garlic and onion in shortening in a skillet until tender. Mix the salt, pepper and flour and dredge the sirloin with seasoned flour. Add to onion mixture and brown. Add the mushrooms, catsup and 1/2 cup bouillon and cover. Simmer for 30 minutes, adding bouillon as needed. Add sour cream and simmer for 30 minutes. Place alternate layers of beef mixture and noodles in a casserole and cover. Refrigerate overnight. Sprinkle with poppy seed. Bake at 325 degrees for 30 minutes, adding bouillon, if needed. 6 servings.

Mrs. Alice Little, Raleigh, North Carolina

BUFFET CASSEROLE

2 15-oz. cans beef ravioli
1/2 lb. beef sirloin
3 tbsp. butter or margarine
1 c. sliced mushrooms
1 10-oz. package frozen
  green beans

1/2 c. beef bouillon
1/2 tsp. salt
1 tsp. flour
2 tbsp. grated Parmesan
  cheese

Preheat oven to 375 degrees. Place the ravioli in 2-tiered row around sides of 8 x 11-inch baking dish. Cut the beef in 2-inch strips. Melt 2 tablespoons butter in a skillet. Add the mushrooms and saute until golden. Remove from skillet. Melt remaining butter in the skillet. Add the beef and brown well. Return mushrooms to skillet and add the green beans, breaking frozen block into pieces. Add the bouillon and salt and bring to a boil. Cover. Cook over low heat for 10 minutes. Mix the flour with enough water to make a thin paste. Stir into liquid in the skillet and cook until thickened. Spoon into center of baking dish and sprinkle cheese over top. Cover. Bake for 25 to 30 minutes. 4-6 servings.

BEEF FRANCAISE

3 lb. boneless beef chuck	1 or 2 bay leaves
Flour	1 lge. onion
3 tsp. salt	4 to 6 whole cloves
1/4 tsp. pepper	10 to 12 sm. onions or potatoes
3 tbsp. shortening or drippings	10 to 12 med. carrots
3 c. water	10 to 12 celery stalks
2 short celery stalks with leaves	2 10-oz. packages frozen peas
1 sprig of thyme (opt.)	1/2 lb. fresh mushrooms, sliced
3 or 4 sprigs of parsley	

Cut the beef in 2-inch cubes. Combine 1/3 cup flour, 2 teaspoons salt and the pepper and dredge beef with seasoned flour. Brown in shortening in a skillet and pour off drippings. Add the water. Tie the celery stalks with leaves, thyme, parsley and bay leaves together for bouquet garni. Stud the large onion with cloves and add bouquet garni and clove-studded onion to the beef. Cover tightly. Bake at 350 degrees for 1 hour and remove bouquet garni and clove-studded onion. Add the small onions. Cut the carrots and celery diagonally in 2-inch pieces and add to beef mixture. Cover and bake for 45 minutes. Add the peas and mushrooms and sprinkle with remaining salt. Cover and bake for 15 to 20 minutes longer or until beef is tender and vegetables are done. Place over low heat and bring to a boil. Thicken with mixture of flour and water. 10-12 servings.

Photograph for this recipe on page 14.

RIGATONI SPECIAL

1 pkg. rigatoni	1 egg
2 to 3 c. minced cooked roast	Salt and pepper to taste
beef	1 can tomato soup
1 lge. onion, minced	2 10 1/2-oz. cans enchilada
2 med. cloves of garlic, minced	sauce

Cook the rigatoni according to package directions and drain. Mix the roast beef, onion, garlic, egg, salt and pepper in a bowl and stuff into rigatoni. Place in lightly greased casserole. Mix the soup and enchilada sauce and pour over stuffed rigatoni. Bake at 350 degrees for 30 minutes. 6-8 servings.

Mrs. Ralph Bailey, Savannah, Georgia

BEEF BURGUNDY

2 lb. beef round	4 tbsp. margarine
Instant meat tenderizer	2 cans beef gravy
1 10-oz. package thin noodles	1/2 pt. sour cream
1 clove of garlic	Salt and pepper to taste
3 med. onions, sliced thin	1/2 c. Burgundy

Cut the beef in 1-inch cubes and sprinkle with tenderizer according to package directions. Cook the noodles according to package directions. Saute garlic and onions in margarine in a skillet over low heat until lightly browned, then discard garlic. Remove onions from skillet. Brown beef cubes in drippings left in skillet and add gravy, sour cream, salt, pepper and onions. Place the noodles in a casserole and pour beef mixture over noodles. Bake in 325-degree oven for 1 hour and 30 minutes or until beef is tender. Add Burgundy and bake for 15 minutes longer. 6 servings.

Mrs. W. L. Wright, Morton, Mississippi

ITALIAN MEAT PIE

1 med. onion, chopped	1/2 c. sliced stuffed olives
2 tbsp. chopped parsley	1/2 c. chopped mushrooms,
3 tbsp. olive oil	drained
3 tbsp. flour	1 tsp. salt
1 1/4 c. water	2 tsp. angostura bitters
1/4 c. tomato paste	Pastry for 2-crust pie
2 c. diced cooked beef	Cream

Saute the onion and parsley in olive oil in a saucepan until onion is tender. Sprinkle with flour. Stir in water and tomato paste and cook over low heat, stirring constantly until smooth and thick. Add the beef, olives, mushrooms, salt and angostura bitters and cool. Line a shallow 1-quart casserole with pastry and fill with beef mixture. Add top crust and cut in several places to allow steam to escape. Flute edges and brush top crust with cream. Bake in 350-degree oven for 45 to 50 minutes or until golden brown.

Mrs. C. Quinn, Opp, Alabama

CLUB DAY CASSEROLE

1 1/2 c. flour	1/2 tsp. marjoram
1 1/2 tsp. seasoned salt	1 tbsp. Worcestershire sauce
1/2 tsp. pepper	2 tsp. parsley flakes
3 lb. stew beef, cut in cubes	3 c. prepared biscuit mix
1/2 c. salad oil	4 tbsp. butter or margarine
1 pkg. onion soup mix	1 c. milk
1 tbsp. powdered mushrooms	

Combine the flour, salt and pepper in a paper bag. Add the beef and shake until coated. Remove beef from bag and reserve remaining flour mixture. Heat the oil in a heavy 2-quart saucepan and brown beef slowly. Add 2 cups water, soup mix, powdered mushrooms, marjoram, Worcestershire sauce and parsley flakes and cover. Cook over low heat for 1 hour. Mix 4 tablespoons reserved flour mixture with 1 cup water and stir into beef mixture. Cook until thickened, stirring constantly, then pour into greased 9 x 13-inch pan. Place the biscuit mix in a bowl and cut in butter. Stir in the milk. Roll out on a floured surface and cut with biscuit cutter. Place on beef mixture. Bake at 400 degrees for 20 minutes or until brown. 8-10 servings.

Mrs. Ralph Tozi, Tallahassee, Florida

Delicious Dividend Casserole (below)

DELICIOUS DIVIDEND CASSEROLE

1/4 c. butter	1 10 1/2-oz. can golden
1 c. sliced celery	mushroom soup
1/4 to 1/2 c. chopped	1/4 c. water
green pepper	Salt and pepper to taste
1/4 c. chopped onion	1/3 c. milk
2 c. diced cooked beef	1/2 c. shredded American
2 tbsp. chopped parsley	process cheese
1 tsp. thyme	1 c. prepared biscuit mix

Melt the butter in a skillet. Add the celery, green pepper and onion and cook for about 15 minutes or until tender. Mix in the beef, parsley and thyme. Add the soup, water, salt and pepper and mix. Place in a casserole. Combine the milk and cheese and add to biscuit mix in a bowl. Stir until well mixed. Knead gently 8 to 10 times on cloth-covered board dusted with additional biscuit mix and roll into rectangle 1/2 inch thick. Cut into 6 squares and place, checkerboard fashion, on top of beef mixture. Bake in 450-degree oven for 10 to 15 minutes or until biscuits are golden brown.

STRIPS OF BEEF CASSEROLE

1 lb. round steak, cut in	1 tbsp. sugar
1/2-in. strips	1 1/2 tsp. salt
1/4 c. shortening	1/2 tsp. pepper
1 1/2 c. chopped onions	1/2 tsp. Worcestershire sauce
2 tbsp. flour	1/2 c. mushrooms
1 c. canned tomatoes	1/2 c. sour cream
1 c. water	1 recipe corn bread batter
1 c. tomato paste	Sesame seed

Brown the steak in shortening in a skillet, stirring occasionally. Add the onions and cook until tender. Stir in the flour. Add tomatoes, water, tomato paste, sugar, salt, pepper and Worcestershire sauce and cover. Simmer for 1 hour and 30 minutes, stirring occasionally. Add the mushrooms and sour cream and simmer for 5 minutes. Place in a 2-quart casserole and top with corn bread batter. Sprinkle with sesame seed. Bake at 425 degrees for 20 to 25 minutes. 6-8 servings.

Mrs. Rena Nell Taylor, Royse City, Texas

POTATO PUFF MEAT PIE

2 c. cubed cooked beef	1/8 tsp. paprika
2 c. gravy	1 tbsp. finely chopped onion
1 tsp. salt	2 c. seasoned mashed potatoes
1/8 tsp. pepper	2 tbsp. butter

Combine the beef, gravy, seasonings and onion and place in a greased casserole. Place mashed potatoes on top and dot with butter. Bake at 450 degrees for 30 minutes or until potatoes are browned. 3-4 servings.

Mrs. Richard E. Hallman, Albuquerque, New Mexico

VENETIAN BEEF PIE

1 1/2 c. flour	1/4 c. grated Parmesan cheese
1 tsp. garlic powder	1/2 c. butter
1 tsp. leaf oregano	4 to 5 tbsp. cold water

Sift the flour with garlic powder into a bowl and add oregano and cheese. Cut in butter until crumbly. Sprinkle with water and stir until mixed. Roll out 2/3 of the pastry on a floured surface into a circle and place in a 1 1/2-quart casserole.

Meat Filling

1 lb. round steak, cut in cubes	1 tsp. sweet basil
1/2 c. flour	1/2 tsp. salt
1/4 c. butter	1/2 tsp. oregano
2 c. tomato sauce	1/2 tsp. garlic
1/4 c. chopped onion	1/8 tsp. pepper
3 tbsp. grated Parmesan cheese	4 slices Cheddar cheese
1 tbsp. sugar	

Dredge the steak with flour and brown in butter in a skillet. Stir in remaining ingredients except cheese slices and cover skillet. Simmer for 30 minutes or until steak is tender. Turn into pastry-lined casserole and top with cheese slices. Roll out remaining dough 1/8 inch thick and cut into 2-inch rounds. Place around edge of casserole, overlapping slightly. Bake at 400 degrees for 30 to 40 minutes or until golden brown. 6-8 servings.

Mrs. Jeanette Knox, Decatur, Alabama

MONDAY MEAT PIE

2 c. cubed cooked roast beef	3/4 c. salad dressing
1 1/2 c. cooked diced potatoes	1 c. boiling water
1 c. cooked diced carrots	1 c. cornmeal
1 tbsp. chopped pimento	1/2 c. milk
1 c. grated mild cheese	1 tbsp. melted butter
1/2 c. chopped onions	2 eggs, well beaten

Combine the roast beef, potatoes, carrots, pimento, cheese, onions and salad dressing in a saucepan and heat until cheese is melted, stirring frequently. Pour into a well-greased casserole. Pour water over cornmeal in a bowl and mix well. Stir in remaining ingredients and pour over beef mixture. Bake at 400 degrees for 40 minutes. 6 servings.

Mrs. Ruby Lee Henry, Ft. Worth, Texas

STEAK WITH DRESSING

Flour	1/8 c. chopped celery
Salt and pepper to taste	1 tbsp. butter
1 round steak, 3/4 in. thick	1 c. long grain rice
Shortening	1 can mushroom soup
1 med. onion, chopped	1 soup can water
1/8 c. chopped bell pepper	1 can whole mushrooms

Mix the flour, salt and pepper and dredge steak with flour mixture. Brown in small amount of shortening in a skillet, then cut in half. Saute the onion, bell pepper and celery in butter in a saucepan until tender. Cook the rice according to package directions and mix with onion mixture. Place half the steak in a casserole and add rice mixture. Cover with remaining steak. Mix the soup with water and pour over steak. Cover casserole. Bake at 350 degrees for 45 minutes. Uncover and add mushrooms. Bake for 15 minutes longer. 4 servings.

Mrs. Jimmie D. Lee, Port Arthur, Texas

BEEF PILAU

1 lb. round or chuck steak	1 1-lb. 4-oz. can red kidney
1 lge. onion, finely chopped	beans
2 tbsp. butter or margarine	1 10 1/2-oz. can beef
2 tsp. salt	consomme
1 c. packaged precooked rice	1 tsp. chili powder
1 1-lb. 4-oz. can tomatoes	1/4 tsp. oregano

Cut the steak in 1-inch cubes. Brown the steak and onion in butter in a skillet and add 1 teaspoon salt. Place alternate layers of steak mixture, rice, tomatoes and beans in a 2-quart casserole. Combine the consomme, chili powder, oregano and remaining salt and pour over beans. Bake at 350 degrees for 1 hour, adding water, as needed, to keep mixture moist. 4-6 servings.

Mrs. T. M. Lamar, Miami, Florida

STUFFED CUBE STEAKS

6 cube steaks	1 lge. can Italian-style
1 pkg. stuffing mix	tomatoes
1 c. cooked rice	Salt and pepper to taste

Place steaks flat and spread stuffing mix almost to edges. Roll steaks and secure with toothpicks. Arrange steaks in a baking dish and cover with rice and tomatoes. Season with salt and pepper. Bake at 350 degrees for 1 hour. 6 servings.

Mrs. Raymond Carter, Santa Fe, New Mexico

MEXICAN BEEF CASSEROLE

2 lb. round steak, 1/2 in. thick	1/8 tsp. minced garlic
	1 No. 2 can tomatoes
Salt and pepper to taste	1 can kidney beans, drained
Chili powder	1/2 tsp. oregano
Prepared mustard	Ground cumin to taste
1 lge. onion, chopped	10 ripe olives, sliced
3 tbsp. salad oil	2 c. bouillon
3/4 lb. long grain rice	

Rub the steak with salt, pepper and 1 tablespoon chili powder. Spread with thin layer of mustard and cut into 1-inch squares. Cook the onion in oil in skillet until golden. Add the rice and cook until brown, stirring constantly. Add garlic. Combine the tomatoes and beans and season with oregano and cumin. Layer half the steak, rice mixture and tomato mixture in greased deep casserole. Sprinkle with chili powder to taste and half the olives. Repeat layers. Add the bouillon and cover. Bake at 350 degrees for 1 hour and 30 minutes or until rice is done. 4 servings.

Marvin A. McGuire, Jr., Richlands, Virginia

SPANISH CASSEROLE WITH RICE

2/3 c. rice	1/4 tsp. paprika
2 tbsp. butter or margarine	1 c. chopped celery
1 med. onion, chopped	1/4 c. chopped green peppers
1 lb. round steak, cut in cubes	1 10 1/2-oz. can tomato soup
3/4 tsp. salt	

Cook the rice according to package directions and set aside. Melt the butter in a skillet and add onion and steak. Season with salt and paprika and cook until brown. Place 1/3 of the rice in a greased baking dish and cover with half the steak mixture. Sprinkle half the celery and green peppers over steak mixture and cover with half the remaining rice. Place remaining steak mixture over rice and sprinkle with remaining celery and green peppers. Cover with remaining rice and pour soup over rice. Cover. Bake at 350 degrees for 30 minutes. 6 servings.

Susan Owens, Clinton, Tennessee

SIRLOIN SUPREME

1 med. sirloin steak	2 cans cream of mushroom soup
2 onions, sliced	1 c. rice
Salt and pepper to taste	

Place steak in a Dutch oven. Place onions over steak and add salt and pepper. Pour soup over all and cover. Bake at 300 degrees for 1 hour. Add rice and mix into soup. Cover and bake for 1 hour longer or until rice is tender.

Shelley Graham, Kilgore, Texas

CHUCK WAGON CASSEROLE

1 1-lb. can whole kernel corn	1 tsp. chili powder
2 c. cubed cooked beef	1 can refrigerator biscuits
1 10 1/2-oz. can tomato soup	2 tbsp. melted butter
1 c. shredded Cheddar cheese	1/4 c. yellow cornmeal
1 tbsp. instant minced onion	

Drain the corn and place in a 2 1/2-quart casserole. Add the beef, soup, cheese, onion and chili powder and mix well. Bake at 400 degrees for 10 minutes. Dip the biscuits in butter, then dip in cornmeal. Place on top of casserole and bake for 20 to 25 minutes longer or until biscuits are golden brown.

Mrs. Clifford Marsh, Jefferson, North Carolina

PASTEL DE CHOCLO

1 lb. chuck steak	2 tbsp. diced ripe olives
1 tbsp. shortening	2 hard-cooked eggs, sliced
1 med. onion, diced	1 No. 303 can whole kernel corn
1 c. meat stock or bouillon	1 tbsp. butter
Salt and red pepper to taste	1/3 c. instant nonfat dry milk
Marjoram to taste	Pinch of sweet basil
Cumin seed to taste	Sugar to taste
1 tbsp. flour	2 eggs, separated
1/4 c. seedless raisins	

Cut the steak in 1-inch cubes. Heat the shortening in a skillet. Add the steak and onion and cook until brown, stirring frequently. Add the meat stock and seasonings and simmer for 30 minutes. Mix the flour with small amount of water and stir into steak mixture. Place in a baking dish and sprinkle raisins, olives and hard-cooked eggs over top. Heat corn and liquid with butter and milk in a saucepan, stirring constantly. Add sweet basil, salt and sugar. Add beaten egg yolks, stirring constantly, then fold in stiffly beaten whites. Pour over steak mixture. Bake at 425 degrees until browned. 6-8 servings.

Mrs. Ramona Morgner, Albuquerque, New Mexico

Swiss Steak with Olive-Tomato Sauce (below)

SWISS STEAK WITH OLIVE-TOMATO SAUCE

1/2 c. flour	1/2 c. sliced stuffed olives
1 1/2 tsp. salt	2 16-oz. cans tomatoes
1/2 tsp. pepper	1 tbsp. bottled thick meat
2 lb. round steak, 1 in. thick	sauce
3 tbsp. shortening	1 bay leaf
2 med. onions, sliced into	1 tsp. light brown sugar
rings	1/8 tsp. thyme leaves

Combine the flour, salt and pepper. Cut the steak in serving pieces and pound flour mixture into steak. Heat the shortening in a large skillet and brown steak in shortening on both sides. Place in a shallow baking dish and cover with onion rings and olives. Place the tomatoes, meat sauce, bay leaf, brown sugar and thyme leaves in a saucepan and bring to boiling point, breaking up tomatoes with the back of a spoon. Pour over the steak and cover. Bake in a 350-degree oven for 1 hour and 30 minutes to 2 hours or until steak is fork-tender. Skim off any excess fat. 6 servings.

BEEF CREOLE

2 1/2 c. mashed potatoes	1/2 green pepper, chopped
3 c. cooked cubed roast beef	2 tomatoes, quartered
or steak	Salt and pepper to taste
1 can beef gravy	

Arrange mashed potatoes around edge of a shallow baking dish. Mix the roast beef with gravy, green pepper, tomatoes and seasonings and pour into center of baking dish. Bake in 400-degree oven until potatoes are brown. 4-5 servings.

Mrs. Roland Joyal, Headland, Alabama

PACKAGE STEAK SUPPER

1 1 1/2-lb. chuck steak, 1 in. thick	2 stalks celery, cut in strips
1 pkg. onion soup mix	3 med. potatoes, halved
1 tsp. steak sauce	2 tbsp. butter or margarine
3 med. carrots, quartered	1/2 tsp. salt

Place the steak in center of a large piece of foil and sprinkle with the soup mix and steak sauce. Cover the steak with vegetables and dot with butter. Sprinkle with salt. Fold foil over steak mixture and seal securely. Place in a baking pan. Bake at 400 degrees for 1 hour to 1 hour and 30 minutes or until done. 4 servings.

Mrs. Dean Wilson, Sarasota, Florida

CASSEROLE OF BEEF

4 c. cooked cubed beef	1/2 c. diced carrots
1/2 tsp. salt	1 c. mushrooms or peas
2 c. brown sauce or gravy	1 onion, thinly sliced
1 tsp. Worcestershire sauce	1 c. small cooked potatoes
1/2 c. diced celery	1 c. canned tomatoes
1/2 tsp. pepper	

Place all ingredients except potatoes and tomatoes in a casserole. Bake at 350 degrees for 1 hour. Add the potatoes and tomatoes and bake for 30 minutes longer. 8 servings.

Mrs. Eugene J. Dumas, Pinellas Park, Florida

CUBE STEAK AND MUSHROOMS

4 cube steaks	2/3 c. buttermilk
4 tbsp. fat	1 tsp. salt
2 med. onions, sliced	1/4 tsp. pepper
1 lb. mushrooms, sliced	4 med. potatoes, sliced
1 can cream of mushroom soup	

Brown the steaks in fat in a skillet and remove from skillet. Saute the onions and mushrooms in the same skillet until tender. Combine the soup, buttermilk and seasonings in a bowl. Place alternate layers of potatoes, onion mixture, steaks and soup mixture in a greased 2 1/2-quart casserole. Bake at 350 degrees for 1 hour. 4 servings.

Mrs. C. B. Herbert, III, Houston, Texas

PRIEST'S LUNCH

3 lb. beef brisket	1 c. diced celery
4 potatoes, diced	8 sm. white onions

3 tomatoes, quartered	4 bay leaves
4 tbsp. chopped parsley	12 whole peppercorns
3 cloves of garlic, minced	2 cans consomme
1 tsp. salt	2 1/2 consomme cans water
2 tbsp. paprika	

Cut the beef brisket in 1-inch cubes. Combine all ingredients in a deep casserole. Cover casserole with foil and tie with string to make a tight seal. Place casserole cover over foil. Bake at 350 degrees for 2 hours and 30 minutes. 6 servings.

Mrs. A. O. Tackett, Charleston, South Carolina

STEAK AND POTATO CASSEROLE

1 lge. round steak	2 tbsp. fat
Salt and pepper to taste	3 to 4 med. potatoes, diced
Flour	1 med. onion, chopped

Cut the steak into serving pieces and sprinkle with salt and pepper. Dredge with flour and brown in fat in a skillet. Place alternate layers of steak, potatoes and onion in a casserole and cover. Bake at 325 degrees for 45 minutes. 4 servings.

Mrs. Jerry McCool, Moss Point, Mississippi

STEAK AND ONION PIE

1 c. sliced onions	1/8 tsp. paprika
1/4 c. shortening	Dash of ginger
1 lb. round steak	Dash of allspice
1/4 c. flour	2 1/2 c. boiling water
2 tsp. salt	2 c. diced potatoes

Fry the onions in shortening in a skillet until tender, then remove from skillet. Cut the steak in small pieces. Mix the flour, seasonings and spices and dredge steak with flour mixture. Brown steak in shortening remaining in the skillet and add boiling water. Cover. Simmer for about 1 hour or until tender. Add the potatoes and cook for 10 minutes longer. Pour into a greased 8-inch casserole and place onions on top.

Egg Pastry

1 c. flour, sifted	1/3 c. shortening
1/2 tsp. salt	1 egg, slightly beaten

Combine the flour and salt in a bowl and cut in shortening until mixture is consistency of large peas. Add the egg and mix thoroughly. Roll out on a floured surface into a circle the size of the casserole and place over steak mixture. Cut several slits for steam to escape and seal edge of pastry. Bake at 450 degrees for 30 minutes.

Mrs. Fred Keever, Kannapolis, North Carolina

BEEF STEW WITH CORN BREAD TOPPING

1/2 tsp. salt	1 med. onion, chopped
3 tbsp. flour	3 potatoes, diced
3/4 lb. beef, cut in 1-in. cubes	1 turnip, diced
1 tbsp. fat	1 stalk celery, diced
	1 recipe corn bread batter

Mix the salt and flour and dredge beef with seasoned flour. Brown in fat in a skillet and cover with water. Simmer until beef is tender. Add the vegetables and cook until vegetables are almost tender. Place in a greased baking dish and cover with corn bread batter. Bake at 350 degrees for 25 minutes. 4-6 servings.

Mary R. Ruble, Newport, Tennessee

HERBED BEEF ROLLS

1 1/2 lb. skirt steak	6 to 8 sm. white onions
Salt and pepper to taste	2 med. potatoes
1 onion, finely chopped	4 carrots
1 tbsp. oregano	4 parsnips or turnips
2 tbsp. oil	1 tbsp. tomato sauce
2 c. (about) beef stock	Cornflour

Cut steak in half lengthwise if thick. Cut steak into 12 pieces and season with salt and pepper. Mix the chopped onion and oregano and sprinkle on steak. Roll up and tie with string. Heat the oil in a skillet and fry steak over high heat until brown. Add enough stock to cover steak and cover the skillet. Simmer for about 1 hour. Peel the onions and cook in boiling water for 5 minutes. Drain. Peel and quarter the potatoes. Peel the carrots and parsnips and cut in 1/2-inch diagonal slices. Add vegetables to steak and add stock to just cover. Stir in tomato sauce, salt and pepper and cover. Bake at 350 degrees until vegetables are tender. Remove steak and vegetables and thicken gravy with cornflour blended with cold water, if necessary. Return steak and vegetables and serve hot. 4 servings.

Photograph for this recipe on cover.

ONION-MEAT PIE

2 c. diced cooked beef	1/2 c. water
1 10-oz. package frozen mixed vegetables	1 pkg. instant potatoes
1 10 1/2-oz. can onion soup	Paprika
2 tbsp. flour	3 tbsp. butter or margarine

Place the beef and mixed vegetables in a 2-quart casserole. Heat the soup in a saucepan. Blend flour and water until smooth and add to soup gradually. Cook until thickened, stirring constantly, then pour over beef mixture. Prepare potatoes according to package directions and spread over beef mixture. Sprinkle with paprika and dot with butter. Bake at 350 degrees for 30 minutes or until potatoes are brown. 4 servings.

Mrs. Albert E. Corey, Crestview, Florida

MEAL-IN-A-CASSEROLE

1 tenderized steak, 1 in. thick	3 lge. carrots, diced
Flour	1 sm. can green beans
Vegetable oil	1 tsp. salt
1 med. cabbage, chopped	1 tsp. pepper
1 med. onion, chopped	1 1/2 c. water
3 lge. potatoes, diced	1 sm. can tomato sauce

Cut steak in serving pieces. Dredge with flour and brown in small amount of hot oil in skillet. Combine the cabbage, onion, potatoes, carrots and beans in a 3-quart casserole and sprinkle with salt and pepper. Combine the water and tomato sauce and pour over vegetables. Place steak on top and cover casserole. Bake at 325 degrees for 1 hour and 15 minutes. 4-6 servings.

Mrs. Emma F. Waggoner, Hennessey, Oklahoma

BARBADOS BEEF STEW

3 lb. beef chuck	1/4 tsp. pepper
3 tbsp. flour	1/3 c. cider vinegar
3 tbsp. fat	1/3 c. unsulphured molasses
1 1-lb. can tomatoes	1 c. water
2 med. onions, sliced	6 carrots, cut in pieces
1 tsp. salt	1/2 c. raisins
1 tsp. celery salt	1/2 tsp. ginger

Cut the beef in 1 1/2-inch cubes and sprinkle with flour. Brown in fat in a heavy saucepan. Add the tomatoes, onions, salt, celery salt and pepper and mix well. Combine the vinegar, molasses and water and add to beef mixture. Cover. Bake at 350 degrees for about 2 hours or until beef is tender. Add the carrots, raisins and ginger and cover. Bake until carrots are tender and serve with mashed potatoes or rice. 12 servings.

Barbados Beef Stew (above)

One-Dish Dinner (below)

ONE-DISH DINNER

1 1/2 c. diagonally sliced celery	1 beef bouillon cube
1/4 c. diced onion	1 10-oz. package frozen mixed vegetables, thawed
1/4 c. butter	1 1-lb. can potatoes, drained
2 tbsp. flour	
2 c. milk	2 c. diced cooked roast beef
1 tsp. salt	1/2 c. corn flake crumbs

Saute the celery and onion in 3 tablespoons butter in a saucepan until tender and stir in the flour. Add the milk, salt and bouillon cube and cook over low heat, stirring constantly, until thickened. Add mixed vegetables. Slice the potatoes and add to celery mixture. Add the beef and pour into a greased 1 1/2-quart casserole. Melt remaining butter, add crumbs and mix well. Sprinkle around edge of casserole. Bake in 350-degree oven for about 30 minutes or until hot and bubbly. 6 servings.

OVEN BEEF STEW

1 1/2 lb. beef, cut in sm. cubes	1 c. diced potatoes (opt.)
1 can tomato sauce	1/4 c. chopped green pepper (opt.)
1 onion, chopped	1 1/2 tsp. salt
1 c. diced carrots	3 tbsp. instant tapioca
1 c. celery, cut in lge. pieces	

Place all ingredients in a casserole and mix well. Cover tightly. Bake at 250 degrees for 5 to 6 hours. 4 servings.

Mrs. C. A. Owens, Ponte Vedra Beach, Florida

BEEF AND OLIVE CASSEROLE

1/2 c. flour	1 lb. small white onions
1 tsp. salt	8 sm. carrots, scraped
1 tsp. pepper	2 10 1/2-oz. cans beef
1/2 tsp. marjoram	bouillon
2 lb. beef chuck, cut in cubes	1 c. stuffed olives, drained
2 tbsp. shortening	Butter

Mix the flour, salt, pepper and marjoram and dredge beef with flour mixture. Brown in shortening in a skillet, then place in a 2-quart casserole. Add the onions, carrots and bouillon and cover. Bake at 350 degrees for about 1 hour and 30 minutes or until beef and vegetables are almost tender. Add the olives and bake for 20 minutes longer. Drain and reserve liquid and pour reserved liquid into a saucepan. Thicken with mixture of 1 tablespoon butter and 1 tablespoon additional flour for each cup of liquid. Pour back into casserole and serve. 6 servings.

Mrs. R. F. Madison, Panama City, Florida

BEEF STROGANOFF

1 1/2 lb. round steak, cut in	1 tsp. salt
sm. cubes	1/2 tsp. pepper
1/4 c. oil	1/4 c. tomato paste
2 c. mushrooms	1 c. consomme
1 c. small onions	1/4 tsp. monosodium glutamate
3 tbsp. flour	Minced garlic to taste
1 bay leaf	1/2 c. sour cream

Brown the steak in oil in a skillet. Add the mushrooms and onions and cook for 5 minutes longer. Stir in flour. Add remaining ingredients except sour cream and place in a casserole. Cover. Bake at 350 degrees for 1 hour. Remove from oven and stir in sour cream. 4-6 servings.

Mrs. Betty Bruce, Tinker Air Force Base, Oklahoma

STUFFED T-BONE STEAKS

2 1-lb. T-bone steaks	1 tbsp. melted butter
1/2 tsp. salt	1/4 tsp. pepper
1 1/2 c. bread or cracker	1 tbsp. water
crumbs	1 tbsp. evaporated milk
1 med. onion, minced	1 egg, beaten
1 tbsp. chopped parsley	

Sprinkle steaks with salt and brown on both sides in small amount of fat in a skillet. Place in a baking dish. Mix the bread crumbs, onion, parsley, butter, pepper, water, milk and egg and place over steaks. Bake at 400 degrees for 30 minutes or until browned.

Cora Mae Jones, Crockett, Texas

VEAL AND EGGPLANT CASSEROLE

2 tbsp. vegetable oil	1/2 tsp. salt
1/4 c. chopped onion	Pepper to taste
1 clove of garlic, minced	2 tbsp. butter
1 16-oz. can stewed tomatoes	1 lb. veal cutlets
1/4 c. tomato paste	1 1/2 lb. eggplant
1/4 tsp. dried oregano leaves	1/3 c. Parmesan cheese
1 1/2 tsp. sugar	

Heat the oil in a saucepan. Add onion and garlic and cook until tender. Add the tomatoes, tomato paste, oregano, sugar, salt and pepper and cover. Simmer for 20 minutes, stirring occasionally. Heat the butter in a skillet and cook the veal cutlets over moderate heat until lightly browned. Pare the eggplant and cut in 1/2-inch slices. Arrange half the eggplant in a 2-quart casserole and top with half the veal cutlets and half the tomato sauce. Repeat layers and sprinkle with cheese. Bake in 350-degree oven for 45 minutes. 4 servings.

Mrs. B. J. Tourville, Atlanta, Georgia

VEAL CHOPS EN CASSEROLE

6 veal rib chops	4 c. thinly sliced potatoes
1 tsp. salt	1/3 c. finely chopped onions
Pepper to taste	1 can cream of mushroom soup
2 tbsp. butter or margarine	1 1/4 c. milk

Season the veal chops with salt and pepper. Melt the butter in a skillet and brown the chops in butter. Place the potatoes in a greased 2-quart baking dish and arrange chops on potatoes. Brown the onions in the same skillet. Add the soup and milk and blend until smooth. Pour over the chops and cover. Bake at 350 degrees for 30 minutes. Uncover and bake for 30 to 40 minutes longer or until potatoes are done. 6 servings.

Mrs. Ralph Chappell, Elkin, North Carolina

VEAL WITH ASPARAGUS

1 1/2 lb. veal cutlets	3/4 c. tomato juice
2 tbsp. shortening	1 tbsp. Marsala
1 pkg. onion soup mix	1 lge. clove of garlic, minced
2 tbsp. flour	1 can asparagus
1 c. water	

Cut the veal cutlets in serving pieces and pound with a meat hammer. Brown in the shortening in a skillet and drain off excess fat. Add the soup mix and flour. Stir in water gradually and place in casserole. Add the tomato juice and Marsala. Add the garlic and asparagus and cover. Bake at 350 degrees for 35 to 40 minutes. 6 servings.

Mrs. B. Eaton, Baltimore, Maryland

Veal-Tamale Pie (below)

VEAL-TAMALE PIE

4 tbsp. butter or margarine	1/2 c. cornmeal
1 1/2 lb. veal shoulder	1 1-lb. can tomatoes
1 sm. onion, chopped	1 1-lb. can cream-style corn
1 garlic clove, chopped	1/2 c. small pitted ripe
2 eggs, beaten	olives
3/4 c. milk	2 tsp. salt
1 tsp. hot sauce	

Melt the butter in a skillet. Cut the veal in 1 1/2-inch cubes and place in butter. Add the onion and garlic and cook over low heat for 15 minutes, stirring occasionally. Turn into a 13 x 9-inch baking dish. Combine the eggs, milk and hot sauce and stir in remaining ingredients. Pour on top of veal mixture and place baking dish in a pan of hot water. Bake in a 325-degree oven for 3 hours. 6 servings.

VEAL AND RICE CASSEROLE

4 slices salt pork, diced	1 c. cooked rice
1 lge. onion, chopped	1 can tomato paste
4 c. cooked diced veal	2 hard-boiled eggs, sliced
Salt and pepper to taste	2 tbsp. butter or margarine
1 c. water	

Fry the salt pork and onion in a skillet until lightly browned. Add the veal, salt, pepper and water and heat through. Pour into well-greased baking dish. Mix the rice and tomato paste and place over veal mixture. Place eggs over rice mixture and dot with butter. Cover. Bake at 350 degrees for 30 minutes, adding small amount of water, if necessary. Tomato soup may be substituted for tomato paste. 4 servings.

Opal Stout, Piedmont, Oklahoma

VEAL HOT DISH

1 lb. veal, cut in cubes	1 can cream of mushroom soup
1 onion, diced	1 can cream of chicken soup
1 tbsp. fat	1/2 c. rice
1 c. chopped celery	1 1/2 tbsp. soy sauce
2 c. water	Salt and pepper to taste

Brown the veal and onion in fat in a skillet. Cook the celery in 1/2 cup water in a saucepan until tender, then add to veal mixture. Add remaining water and remaining ingredients and mix well. Place in a baking dish. Bake at 350 degrees for 2 hours. 4 servings.

Mrs. Robert Chesbrough, Vero Beach, Florida

VENETIAN VEAL

1 lb. veal steak, 1/2 in. thick	1/2 tsp. salt
	1/8 tsp. pepper
1/2 c. butter	1 c. milk
1/2 c. chopped celery	1/4 tsp. thyme
1/4 c. chopped onion	1/4 tsp. basil
1/4 c. chopped carrots	1/8 tsp. marjoram
1 4-oz. can sliced mushrooms	2 tbsp. chopped parsley
2 tbsp. flour	1 6-oz. can tomato paste

Preheat oven to 350 degrees. Brown the veal in 1/4 cup butter in a skillet and remove from skillet. Cut in strips and place in a greased 1 1/4-quart casserole. Add remaining butter to drippings in skillet. Saute the celery, onion, carrots and drained mushrooms in skillet. Remove with a slotted spoon and place over veal in casserole. Pour off all except 2 tablespoons butter from skillet and stir in flour, salt and pepper. Add milk gradually and cook, stirring, until smooth and slightly thickened. Add remaining ingredients and stir until blended. Pour over vegetables in casserole. Bake for about 1 hour and serve with buttered noodles. 4 servings.

Venetian Veal (above)

Season the
frying pan.
until brow
the tomato
minutes. C
until brow
Bake for 4
Sprinkle w
servings.

GREEN I

1 1/2 lb
thick
1/2 c. b
1 tsp. sa
1/4 tsp.
1 6-oz.
1 c. coa
1 tbsp.

Cut the ve
with 1/2 te
reserved m
40 minutes
and saute
mushrooms
heated thro
to veal mi
2-quart sha
Sprinkle ar
or until hea

Green Bean-

VEAL SUPREME

1 1/2 lb. veal, cut in cubes	1 green pepper, diced
1 sm. onion, chopped	Salt and pepper to taste
2 tbsp. butter or margarine	1 12-oz. package noodles
1 can mushroom soup	2 c. shredded sharp cheese
1 sm. can mushrooms	Buttered bread crumbs
1 c. sour cream	

Saute the veal and onion in butter in a skillet until brown. Add small amount of water and simmer until tender. Add the soup, mushrooms, sour cream, green pepper, salt and pepper and blend well. Prepare the noodles according to package directions. Place alternate layers of noodles, veal mixture and cheese in a shallow casserole and cover with crumbs. Bake at 350 degrees for 45 minutes. 8 servings.

Mrs. David E. Turner, New Orleans, Louisiana

CHINESE VEAL CASSEROLE

1/2 c. chopped onions	2 c. water
1 1/2 lb. veal, cut in cubes	1/8 c. soy sauce
1 tbsp. shortening or olive oil	1/2 tsp. salt
1 c. sliced celery	1/8 tsp. pepper
1/2 c. rice	1 pkg. frozen peas, thawed
1/2 c. cream of mushroom soup	1/2 c. blanched slivered
1/2 c. cream of chicken soup	almonds
1 sm. can mushrooms	

Saute the onions and veal in shortening until browned, then place in a casserole. Mix in the celery, rice, soups, mushrooms, water, soy sauce, salt and pepper and cover. Bake at 350 degrees for 45 minutes. Stir in peas and cover. Bake for 30 minutes. Remove cover and sprinkle with almonds. Bake for 15 minutes longer or until almonds are brown. 8 servings.

Mrs. Lloyd P. Smith, Arkadelphia, Arkansas

VEAL A LA KING

2 lb. veal, cut in 1-in. cubes	1 can mushrooms
Shortening	1 green pepper, finely chopped
1 lge. onion, chopped	4 whole cloves
6 carrots, diced	2 bay leaves
1 can peas	6 c. thick white sauce

Brown the veal in small amount of shortening in a skillet. Add the onion and brown. Place in a casserole and add the carrots, peas, mushrooms and green pepper. Tie the cloves and bay leaves in a cheesecloth bag and place in casserole. Bake at 300 degrees for 2 hours. Remove spice bag and stir in white sauce. Serve on heated chow mein noodles or in patty shells. 8-10 servings.

Mrs. Jimmy Thomas, Palm Beach, Florida

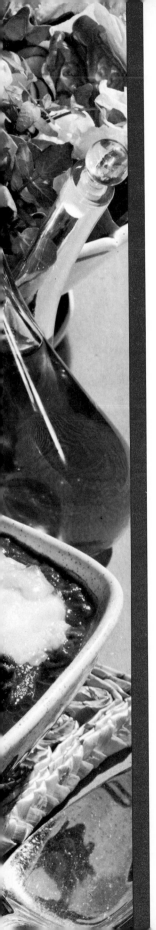

ground beef

Ground beef is a boon to every homemaker! With it she can balance her budget while preparing quick and easy family-pleasing dishes. And with it she transforms vegetables and pasta into marvelous casseroles.

Here, in the pages of the section that follows, you'll find an unusual selection of recipes from the kitchens of southern homemakers — recipes that show you imaginative new ways to turn ground beef into casseroles.

There are Italian-style recipes, such as the one for Ravioli, little meat-filled pies so perfect for luncheons or supper. For a special treat, try Tagliarini, a palate-pleasing mixture of ground beef, onions, peppers, corn, and mushrooms.

Then there are recipes for hearty ground beef pies. Beef and Vegetables in Cheese Pastry combines the rich flavors of tomatoes, carrots, and potatoes with ground beef and a rich sauce. This delectable casserole is topped off with a cloud-light layer of cheese puff pastry — utterly delicious!

Ground beef with vegetables . . . pasta . . . rice . . . recipes for all these variations abound in the following section. Every recipe has been perfected by a southern homemaker. These creative cooks now share their favorite recipes with you, hoping that you will take as much pleasure in serving these dishes as they have in developing them.

39

BEEF AND BEAN CASSEROLE

1 lb. ground beef	**1/4 c. (packed) brown sugar**
1 lge. onion, chopped	**1 tbsp. prepared mustard**
1 1-qt. can red kidney beans	**Salt and pepper to taste**
1 can tomato soup	**Sliced bacon (opt.)**

Brown the ground beef and onion in a frypan and drain. Add remaining ingredients except bacon and mix well. Place in a baking dish and cover top with bacon. Bake at 350 degrees for 1 hour. Pork and beans may be substituted for kidney beans.

Roma Bettridge, Dallas Texas

CHEESEY BUN BEEFEROLE

1 lb. ground beef	**1 10-oz. package frozen**
1/4 c. sliced onion	**lima beans**
1 clove of garlic, minced	**1 1/2 slices process cheese**
1 tsp. chili powder	**1 8-oz. package refrigerator**
1 10 3/4-oz. can beef gravy	**biscuits**

Cook the ground beef, onion, garlic and chili powder in a skillet until beef is browned and pour off fat. Stir in gravy. Cook the lima beans according to package directions and drain. Add to beef mixture and heat to boiling point. Place in a 1 1/2-quart casserole. Cut the cheese into 6 squares and place 1 biscuit around each square, pinching ends. Place around edge of casserole. Bake at 425 degrees for 15 to 20 minutes. Bake remaining biscuits according to package directions and serve with casserole.

Cheesey Bun Beeferole (above)

MEXICAN CORN BREAD AND BEEF

1 lb. ground beef
1 1/8 c. yellow cornmeal
1/2 tsp. soda
2 eggs
1 c. milk
3/4 tsp. salt
1/2 c. bacon drippings

1 No. 2 can cream-style yellow
  corn
4 canned jalapeno peppers,
  chopped
1/2 lb. longhorn cheese, grated
1 lge. onion, chopped

Cook the beef in a skillet until brown and drain. Mix 1 cup cornmeal and soda in a bowl. Add the eggs, milk, salt, corn and bacon drippings and mix well. Place remaining cornmeal in a greased skillet and brown. Pour half the corn bread mixture into skillet and add beef. Sprinkle with the jalapeno peppers, cheese and onion. Pour remaining corn bread mixture over onion. Bake at 350 degrees for 45 minutes or until done. 6-8 servings.

Mrs. D. C. Leonard, Olustee, Oklahoma

CHEESE POLENTA

1 c. farina or cornmeal
1 qt. hot milk
2 tsp. butter
1 tsp. salt

1 egg, beaten
1 c. shredded sharp American
  cheese

Add the farina slowly to hot milk, stirring constantly. Add the butter and salt and cook, stirring occasionally, in a double boiler, for 15 to 20 minutes or until thickened. Add the egg and cheese and stir until cheese is melted. Pour into a greased 8-inch square baking dish and chill until firm.

Sauce

1/2 c. finely chopped onion
1 clove of garlic, minced
1 tbsp. butter
1/2 lb. ground beef
1 c. sliced fresh mushrooms
1/2 tsp. salt

1 No. 303 can tomatoes
1 6-oz. can tomato paste
1 tsp. sugar
1/2 tsp. oregano
1 c. shredded sharp American
  cheese

Cook the onion and garlic in butter in a saucepan until transparent. Add the ground beef and cook, stirring, until partially done. Add the mushrooms and cook until tender. Add the salt, tomatoes, tomato paste and sugar and cover. Simmer for 2 hours, adding small amount of water if necessary. Add the oregano and cook until flavors are blended. Cut farina mixture into small squares and place in a large, shallow baking dish or individual baking dishes. Cover with sauce and sprinkle with cheese. Bake in a 325-degree oven for 15 to 20 minutes or until cheese is melted and mixture is heated thoroughly. 5-6 servings.

Photograph for this recipe on page 38.

GOLD NUGGET MEAT PIE

1 c. soft bread crumbs	3 tbsp. catsup
1/2 c. milk	1/4 c. chopped onion
3/4 lb. ground round steak	2 tbsp. butter or margarine
1 egg, beaten	1 12-oz. can whole kernel
2 tbsp. grated onion	corn
2 tsp. salt	1 c. drained tomatoes
1 tbsp. Worcestershire sauce	1/2 tsp. basil

Soften the bread crumbs in milk in a large mixing bowl. Add the ground steak, egg, grated onion, 1 teaspoon salt, Worcestershire sauce and catsup and mix well. Line bottom and side of an 8-inch casserole with steak mixture. Bake at 350 degrees for 40 minutes. Cook the chopped onion in butter in a saucepan until golden. Drain the corn and add to the onion. Add the tomatoes, remaining salt and basil and simmer for 10 minutes. Place in baked steak mixture. Bake for 15 minutes longer and garnish with parsley. 6 servings.

Marlene Green, Jacksboro, Texas

SQUAW CORN

1 lb. ground beef	2 eggs, beaten
2 tbsp. shortening	1/4 c. milk
1 1/2 tsp. salt	1 1/2 c. soft bread crumbs
1/2 tsp. dried thyme	1 1-lb. can cream-style corn
1/4 tsp. dried marjoram	2 tsp. prepared mustard
1/4 c. chopped onion	2 tbsp. melted butter

Brown the beef in shortening in a skillet. Add the seasonings, onion, eggs, milk, 1 cup crumbs, corn and mustard and mix well. Place in a greased 2-quart casserole. Mix remaining crumbs and butter and sprinkle over beef mixture. Bake at 350 degrees for 30 to 40 minutes. 8 servings.

Wiley B. Greer, Marion, Virginia

CORN BREAD PIE

1 lb. ground beef	1/2 c. chopped green pepper
1 lge. onion, chopped	3/4 c. yellow cornmeal
1 can tomato soup	1 tbsp. sugar
2 c. water	1 tbsp. flour
1 1/2 tsp. salt	1 1/2 tsp. baking powder
3/4 tsp. pepper	1 beaten egg
1 tbsp. chili powder	1/2 c. milk
1 c. whole kernel corn, drained	1 tbsp. melted fat

Brown the beef and onion in a skillet. Add the soup, water, 1 teaspoon salt, pepper, chili powder, corn and green pepper and mix well. Simmer for 15 minutes and pour into a greased casserole. Sift the cornmeal, sugar, flour, remaining salt and baking powder into a bowl. Add the egg and milk and stir lightly. Add the fat and mix. Spread over beef mixture. Bake at 350 degrees for 18 to 20 minutes. 6-8 servings.

Mrs. Robert O. Adamson, Fort Seybert, West Virginia

TAMALE-CHEESE PIE

1/2 c. chopped onion	1 tbsp. chili powder
1 clove of garlic, minced	2 1/2 tsp. salt
2 tbsp. butter	1 c. sliced pitted black
1/2 lb. ground beef	olives
1 c. sliced mushrooms	3/4 c. cornmeal
1 1-lb. can tomatoes	3 c. milk
1 12-oz. can whole kernel	2 eggs, beaten
corn, drained	2 c. shredded sharp Cheddar
1 8-oz. can tomato sauce	cheese
1/4 c. chopped green pepper	

Saute the onion and garlic in 1 tablespoon butter until tender. Add beef and mushrooms and cook, stirring, until beef loses red color. Add the tomatoes, corn, tomato sauce, green pepper, chili powder and 1 1/2 teaspoons salt and cover. Simmer for about 45 minutes. Add the olives and simmer for 15 minutes longer. Mix the cornmeal and 1 cup milk. Combine remaining milk, butter and salt in a saucepan and heat to boiling point. Add cornmeal mixture gradually and cook, stirring constantly, until thickened. Cover and cook over very low heat for about 15 minutes. Stir in eggs and 1 cup cheese and stir until cheese is melted. Line bottom of greased 2-quart shallow casserole with cornmeal mixture, reserving 1 1/2 cups for top of pie. Pour beef mixture over cornmeal mixture. Drop reserved cornmeal mixture by spoonfuls on top of beef mixture and sprinkle remaining cheese over top. Bake at 350 degrees for 50 to 60 minutes or until browned and bubbly. 6-8 servings.

Tamale-Cheese Pie (above)

Beef and Corn Bread Supper (below)

BEEF AND CORN BREAD SUPPER

1 1/2 lb. ground beef	1/2 c. cornmeal
1 10 1/2-oz. can cream of asparagus soup	1 tbsp. baking powder
	1 tsp. salt
1/4 c. finely chopped onion	1/4 c. melted shortening
2 tsp. Worcestershire sauce	2/3 c. milk
3/4 c. sifted all-purpose flour	6 green pepper rings

Preheat oven to 425 degrees. Brown the ground beef in a 10-inch cast iron skillet. Add the soup, onion and Worcestershire sauce and simmer for about 5 minutes. Sift the flour, cornmeal, baking powder and salt together into a medium bowl. Add the shortening and milk and beat until smooth. Pour over the ground beef mixture and spread with narrow spatula to within 1/2 inch of edge. Top with green pepper rings. Bake for 15 to 20 minutes. 6 servings.

TAGLIARINI

1 1/2 lb. ground beef	1/2 pkg. egg noodles
1 lge. onion, chopped	1 can cream-style corn
1 chopped green pepper	1 can mushrooms
2 cans tomato paste or sauce	1 c. grated Cheddar cheese

Place the ground beef in a baking dish and add onion. Add green pepper and tomato paste. Cook the noodles according to package directions and place over tomato paste. Add the corn, then add mushrooms. Cover with cheese. Bake at 350 degrees for 1 hour. 6 servings.

Judith Ogle, Tahlequah, Oklahoma

GROUND BEEF-EGGPLANT CASSEROLE

6 tbsp. butter	1 1/2 c. canned tomatoes
5 c. diced eggplant	1 c. grated cheese
2 c. cooked ground beef	Salt and pepper to taste
2 onions, sliced	1 c. fine dry bread crumbs

Melt 3 tablespoons butter in a skillet and add the eggplant. Cook over low heat for 5 minutes. Place alternate layers of eggplant, ground beef, onions, tomatoes and 3/4 cup cheese in a greased casserole, seasoning each layer with salt and pepper. Mix the bread crumbs with remaining cheese and sprinkle over casserole. Dot with remaining butter. Bake at 375 degrees for about 35 minutes or until browned. 5 servings.

Mrs. Yancey Cook, Phoenix, Arizona

EGGPLANT FESTIVE

3 tbsp. butter	1 c. tomato sauce
1 lb. lean ground beef	1 c. water
1 med. onion, finely chopped	Salt and pepper to taste
1/4 c. pine nuts	1 med. eggplant

Melt the butter in a skillet. Add the ground beef and cook until partially done. Add the onion, pine nuts, tomato sauce, water, salt and pepper and simmer for 15 minutes. Peel the eggplant and cut in 1/4-inch thick slices. Place 1/3 of the eggplant in 8 x 10-inch casserole. Add half the beef mixture and cover with half the remaining eggplant. Add remaining beef mixture, then add remaining eggplant. Cover. Bake at 325 degrees for 30 minutes or until eggplant is tender. 6 servings.

Mrs. Carmen Kazen Ferris, Austin, Texas

BEEF AND VEGETABLES IN CHEESE PASTRY

1 lb. ground beef	1 c. diced cooked carrots
1/4 c. chopped onion	1 c. diced cooked potatoes
1/4 c. shortening	1 tsp. Worcestershire sauce
1 1/8 c. all-purpose flour	1 1/2 tsp. baking powder
1 1/2 tsp. salt	1/2 tsp. dry mustard
1/4 tsp. pepper	1/4 c. grated sharp cheese
2 c. cooked tomatoes	1/2 c. milk

Brown the ground beef and onion in half the shortening in a skillet, then stir in 2 tablespoons flour, 1 teaspoon salt and pepper. Add the tomatoes, carrots, potatoes and Worcestershire sauce and cook over medium heat until thickened, stirring frequently. Pour into a greased 2-quart casserole. Place remaining flour, baking powder, remaining salt and mustard in a bowl and stir well. Cut in remaining shortening and cheese with pastry blender until mixture resembles coarse meal. Add the milk and stir just until dry ingredients are moistened. Spread on beef mixture. Bake at 425 degrees for 18 to 20 minutes.

Mrs. Marilyn Kuhn, Giddings, Texas

HAMBURGER PATTIES CASSEROLE

6 hamburger patties	**1 1/2 tsp. salt**
2 med. onions, sliced	**1 13 1/2-oz. can tomatoes**
5 med. potatoes, sliced	

Place 3 hamburger patties in a 2-quart casserole and add half the onions. Add half the potatoes and repeat layers. Add the salt and pour tomatoes over top. Cover. Bake at 350 degrees for 30 minutes or until done. 6 servings.

Mrs. Kenneth Perry, Joelton, Tennessee

BEEF AND POTATO CASSEROLE

4 c. cooked ground beef	**1/2 c. barbecue sauce**
4 c. mashed potatoes	**Salt and pepper to taste**
1 lge. onion, grated	**3/4 c. grated cheese**
2 eggs, beaten	**1/2 c. catsup**

Combine the ground beef, potatoes, onion, eggs, barbecue sauce, salt and pepper and mix well. Press into a casserole. Place cheese on top and pour catsup over cheese. Cover. Bake at 350 degrees for 20 minutes. Uncover and bake for 10 minutes longer.

Mrs. Louise Davis, Houston, Texas

MEATBALL-MUSHROOM CASSEROLE

2 lb. ground beef	**3/4 tsp. salt**
1 egg	**1 can cream of mushroom soup**
1/2 c. bread crumbs	**3/4 c. milk**
1/2 tsp. onion powder	**1 can peas and onions**
1/2 tsp. seasoned salt	**2 lb. cooked potatoes, mashed**
Pepper to taste	**Paprika**

Combine the ground beef, egg, crumbs and seasonings and shape into large meatballs. Brown in a skillet over high heat and place in a large casserole. Blend the soup and milk in pan drippings in the skillet and over meatballs. Bake at 350 degrees for 20 minutes. Drain the peas and onions and place in the casserole. Bake for 10 minutes longer. Mound potatoes around edge of casserole and sprinkle with paprika. Increase temperature to 450 degrees and bake until potatoes are brown. 8 servings.

Mrs. Charles Griffin, San Antonio, Texas

BAKED LASAGNA SUPREME

1 lge. onion, diced	**1 No. 2 1/2 can tomatoes**
1 clove of garlic, minced	**1 6-oz. can tomato paste**
1 lb. ground beef, crumbled	**1 tbsp. chopped parsley**
1/2 c. olive oil	**3 bay leaves**

1 tsp. sweet basil	1 pkg. mozzarella cheese
1/4 tsp. crushed red pepper	1 carton ricotta cheese
1 1-lb. package lasagna	1 pkg. grated Parmesan cheese

Cook the onion, garlic and beef in olive oil in a skillet until brown, stirring frequently. Place the tomatoes, tomato paste, parsley, bay leaves, basil and red pepper in a heavy saucepan and simmer for several minutes. Add the beef mixture and simmer for 3 hours. Cook the lasagna according to package directions and drain well. Layer the beef sauce, lasagna, mozzarella cheese, ricotta cheese and Parmesan cheese in 3-quart casserole until all ingredients are used, ending with noodles and beef sauce. Bake at 350 degrees for 30 minutes. Cottage cheese may be substituted for ricotta cheese. 8 servings.

Mrs. Peter Gordon, Paducah, Kentucky

BEEF-PARMESAN CASSEROLE

1 1/2 lb. lean ground beef	1/2 tsp. sweet basil
1 lge. green pepper, chopped	1/2 tsp. celery seed
2 onions, chopped	1 tsp. brown sugar
3 sm. cans tomato sauce	1 tsp. mustard
1 sm. can tomato paste	Salt and pepper to taste
1 sm. can mushrooms	1 8-oz. package egg noodles
1/2 tsp. oregano	Grated Parmesan cheese
1 bay leaf	

Brown the beef, green pepper and onions in a heavy skillet and add remaining ingredients except noodles and cheese. Bring to a boil and cover. Simmer for 3 to 4 hours. Cook the noodles according to package directions and drain. Place alternate layers of noodles and beef sauce in large, deep casserole and top with Parmesan cheese. Bake at 350 degrees for 15 minutes. 6-8 servings.

Mrs. E. L. Purcell, Charlotte, North Carolina

BEEF-WATER CHESTNUT CASSEROLE

1 lb. ground beef	1 can cream of celery soup
Salt and pepper to taste	1 sm. can evaporated milk
1 med. onion, chopped	1 can water chestnuts, sliced
1/2 green pepper, finely chopped	1 sm. jar pimentos, chopped
	1 c. bread crumbs
1 8-oz. box fine noodles	Butter

Season the ground beef with salt and pepper. Cook the beef, onion and green pepper in a skillet until brown. Cook the noodles according to package directions and add to beef mixture. Mix the soup and milk and add to beef mixture. Add the water chestnuts and pimentos and mix well. Place in a casserole. Sprinkle with bread crumbs and dot with butter. Bake at 350 degrees for 30 minutes. 6-8 servings.

Mrs. Helen Lee, Falls Church, Virginia

Beef-Stuffed Rigatoni (below)

BEEF-STUFFED RIGATONI

1 12-oz. package rigatoni	1 tsp. mixed Italian herbs
1 9-oz. package frozen chopped spinach	3/4 c. grated Parmesan cheese
1/3 c. chopped onion	1 14 1/2-oz. can Italian tomatoes
1/3 c. chopped green pepper	1 8-oz. can tomato sauce
1 clove of garlic, minced	1 3-oz. can mushrooms
1 tbsp. cooking oil	1 8-oz. package sliced mozzarella cheese
1 1/2 lb. ground beef chuck	
1 1/2 tsp. salt	

Cook the rigatoni in 4 quarts boiling, salted water for about 8 minutes or until just tender. Drain and cover with cold water. Cook the spinach according to package directions and drain, pressing out all liquid. Cook the onion, green pepper and garlic in oil in a skillet until soft. Add the ground beef, salt and herbs and cook until beef is brown. Combine 2/3 of the beef mixture with spinach and 1/4 cup Parmesan cheese and reserve. Add the tomatoes, tomato sauce and mushrooms to remaining beef mixture in skillet and cook over low heat, stirring occasionally, until thickened. Drain the rigatoni and stuff each piece with reserved spinach mixture. Place layers of beef sauce, stuffed rigatoni, mozzarella cheese and remaining Parmesan cheese in a 9-inch casserole, ending with beef sauce and cheese. Bake at 350 degrees for 30 to 40 minutes or until hot and bubbly. 8 servings.

SPANISH NOODLES

1 lge. onion, chopped	1 can English peas
1 tbsp. oil	1 1/2 cans tomato soup
3/4 pkg. noodles	Chili powder to taste
1 1/2 lb. hamburger, crumbled	

Cook the onion in oil in a saucepan until tender. Cook the noodles according to package directions. Brown the hamburger in a skillet. Place alternate layers of hamburger, onion, peas, noodles and soup in a 2-quart casserole and sprinkle with chili powder. Cover. Bake at 350 degrees for 45 minutes. 6 servings.

Mrs. N. R. Weatherall, Tutwiler, Mississippi

JIFFY BEEF STROGANOFF

1 lb. ground beef	3 1/2 c. hot water
1/2 pkg. onion soup mix	2 tbsp. flour
1/2 tsp. ginger	1 c. sour cream
3 c. medium noodles	2 tbsp. sherry (opt.)
1 3-oz. can sliced mushrooms	

Brown the ground beef in 2 tablespoons fat in a skillet and sprinkle with soup mix and ginger. Add the noodles, mushrooms and liquid and water. Place in a casserole and cover tightly. Bake at 350 degrees for 1 hour or until noodles are done. Blend flour into sour cream and stir into beef mixture. Bake for 5 minutes longer or until thickened. Add sherry just before serving. 4-6 servings.

Mrs. J. A. Bagwell, West Memphis, Arkansas

JACKPOT

1 lb. ground beef	1 No. 2 can red kidney beans
1/4 c. chopped onion	1 1/2 c. grated cheese
1 can tomato soup	Salt and pepper to taste
1 1/2 soup cans water	Chili powder to taste
4 oz. wide noodles	

Brown the beef with onion in a skillet. Add soup, water and noodles and cover. Cook until noodles are tender. Add beans, 1/2 of the cheese and seasonings and pour into a casserole. Sprinkle with remaining cheese. Bake at 350 degrees for 45 minutes. 8 servings.

Mrs. J. C. Lindsay, Oklahoma City, Oklahoma

CASSEROLE ITALIANO

1 lb. ground beef	1 can tomato soup
1/4 c. chopped onion	1/2 soup can water
1 med. clove of garlic, minced	2 c. cooked wide noodles
1/2 tsp. salt	1 c. shredded cheese
1/2 tsp. oregano	

Brown the beef with onion, garlic, salt and oregano in a skillet, stirring frequently. Add the soup, water and noodles. Pour into a 1 1/2-quart casserole and place cheese around edge. Bake at 350 degrees for 30 minutes. 8 servings.

Mrs. G. A. Shields, Decatur, Texas

SHORTCUT LASAGNA

1 lb. ground beef	1 8-oz. package lasagna
3 1/2 c. canned tomatoes	1 8-oz. package sliced
1 c. seasoned tomato sauce	mozzarella cheese
2 env. spaghetti sauce mix	1 c. cream-style cottage cheese
2 cloves of garlic, minced	1/2 c. grated Parmesan cheese
Salt to taste	

Brown the beef in a skillet and drain off excess fat. Add the tomatoes, tomato sauce, sauce mix and garlic and simmer for 40 minutes, stirring occasionally. Add the salt. Cook the lasagna according to package directions. Drain and rinse in cold water. Layer 1/2 of the lasagna, 1/3 of the beef sauce, 1/2 of the mozzarella cheese and 1/2 of the cottage cheese in casserole and repeat layers, ending with beef sauce. Top with Parmesan cheese. Bake at 350 degrees for 25 to 30 minutes. Let stand for 15 minutes and cut into squares. 6-8 servings.

Mary Nan Fitch, Electra, Texas

MEAT-FILLED MANICOTTI

1 can tomato paste	2 tbsp. cooking oil
1 lge. can tomatoes	1 pkg. grated mozzarella cheese
1/2 tsp. basil	1/4 c. bread crumbs
1/2 tsp. oregano	1/2 tsp. salt
1 clove of garlic, chopped (opt.)	Dash of pepper
1/2 lb. ground beef	1 pkg. manicotti
2 tbsp. chopped onion	1/4 c. grated Romano cheese
2 tbsp. chopped green pepper	

Mix the tomato paste, tomatoes, basil, oregano and garlic. Brown the ground beef, onion and green pepper in oil in a skillet. Drain off excess oil and cool. Add the mozzarella cheese, crumbs, salt, pepper and 2 tablespoons tomato sauce. Cook the manicotti according to package directions until partially done and drain well. Fill manicotti with beef mixture. Pour small amount of tomato sauce into a casserole and arrange manicotti in sauce. Cover with remaining sauce and cover the casserole. Bake at 400 degrees for 45 minutes, then sprinkle with Romano cheese. 6 servings.

Mrs. D. M. Ford, Anniston, Alabama

RAVIOLI

1/2 lb. shell macaroni	1/3 tsp. basil
1 pkg. frozen chopped spinach	1/2 tsp. rosemary
1 med. onion, diced	Salt and pepper to taste
2 cloves of garlic, minced	2 eggs, well beaten
2 tbsp. shortening	1/2 c. bread crumbs
1 lb. ground beef	1 c. grated Cheddar cheese
1 6-oz. can tomato paste	1/2 c. salad oil
1 8-oz. can tomato sauce	1 can mushroom soup
1/3 tsp. oregano	

Cook the macaroni according to package directions and drain. Cook the spinach according to package directions and drain, reserving 3/4 cup liquid. Saute the onion and 1 clove of garlic in shortening until tender. Add the beef and cook until well browned. Add reserved spinach liquid, tomato paste, tomato sauce, herbs, salt and pepper and simmer for 15 to 20 minutes. Mix the spinach, eggs, bread crumbs, cheese, remaining garlic, oil and salt. Place alternate layers of macaroni, spinach mixture and beef mixture in 9 x 13-inch casserole and cool. Cover with plastic wrap and refrigerate for 24 hours. Remove plastic wrap and pour mushroom soup over top. Bake at 350 degrees for 30 to 40 minutes. 10 servings.

Mrs. Riley Henderson, Gulfport, Mississippi

MACARONI CHILI

2 lb. ground round	1/2 tsp. oregano leaves
3 tbsp. olive or salad oil	1/2 tsp. pepper
1 1-lb. 12-oz. can tomatoes	1 bay leaf
1 qt. tomato juice	1 15-oz. can red kidney
2 c. chopped onions	beans, drained
3 cloves of garlic, minced	1 c. chopped sweet mixed
Salt	pickles
2 tbsp. chili powder	3 qt. boiling water
1/2 tsp. ground cumin seed	2 c. elbow macaroni

Brown the ground round in oil in a Dutch oven, stirring frequently. Add the tomatoes, tomato juice, onions, garlic, 4 teaspoons salt and remaining seasonings and cover. Bake at 350 degrees for 1 hour. Stir in the kidney beans and pickles and bake for 30 minutes longer. Remove the bay leaf. Add 1 tablespoon salt to boiling water in a saucepan and add macaroni gradually so water continues to boil. Cook, stirring occasionally, until tender and drain in a colander. Combine with chili and serve in individual bowls. 10 servings.

Macaroni Chili (above)

BEEF-MACARONI SUPERB

1 8-oz. package shell macaroni	1 tomato puree can water
1 lb. ground beef	1 can mushroom soup
1 med. onion, chopped	1/2 tsp. salt
1 green pepper, chopped	1/2 lb. American cheese, cubed
1/2 c. sliced stuffed olives	1/2 c. bread crumbs
1 can tomato puree	

Cook the macaroni according to package directions. Brown the beef in a skillet. Add the onion, green pepper and olives and cook until onion is tender. Add tomato puree, water, soup, macaroni, salt and cheese and place in a casserole. Sprinkle with crumbs. Bake at 325 degrees for 30 minutes. 8-10 servings.

Mrs. Josephine S. Loyd, Oneonta, Alabama

JIFFY CASSEROLE

1 8-oz. package elbow macaroni	1 lb. ground beef
2 sm. cans tomato paste	Salt and pepper to taste
1 c. chopped onion	1 c. grated cheese
1 No. 2 can whole kernel corn	

Cook the macaroni according to package directions and place in a greased casserole. Add 1 can tomato paste and cover with onion. Add the corn and pour remaining tomato paste over corn. Mix the ground beef with salt and pepper and place over tomato paste. Bake at 350 degrees until beef is done. Cover with cheese and bake until cheese melts.

Mrs. Roy J. Roach, Jr., Chatham, Virginia

GROUND STEAK CASSEROLE

2 lge. onions, chopped	1/3 10-oz. package macaroni
2 tbsp. margarine	Salt and pepper to taste
1 green pepper, chopped	2 c. canned tomatoes
1 lb. ground round steak	3/4 c. grated sharp cheese
1/2 c. chopped celery	

Cook the onions in the margarine in a saucepan until soft. Add the green pepper, ground steak, celery, macaroni, salt, pepper, tomatoes and half the cheese. Place in a shallow casserole and add remaining cheese. Refrigerate overnight. Bake at 350 degrees for 1 hour. 6-8 servings.

Mrs. Roy Hayes, Dumas, Texas

FRENCH HUNTERS' DINNER CASSEROLE

1 lb. hamburger	1 clove of garlic, minced
1 onion, chopped	Pepper to taste
1/2 tsp. chili powder	1 can tomato soup

1 can spaghetti

1 sm. can mushrooms

1 can lima beans, drained

1 can Chinese vegetables

1 c. grated cheese

1 c. crushed potato chips

Brown the hamburger and onion in a skillet. Add remaining ingredients except cheese and potato chips and place in a casserole. Cover with cheese and potato chips. Bake in 350-degree oven until heated through and cheese is melted. One-half teaspoon garlic salt may be substituted for garlic.

Mrs. Virgil Lindley, Paragould, Arkansas

BEEF-FARCE RISOTTO

1 yellow onion, chopped fine

2 tbsp. margarine

1 lb. ground beef, crumbled

1 c. rice

1 can peeled tomatoes

2 c. water

1 1/2 tsp. salt

Freshly ground pepper to taste

1 or 2 red or green peppers

Fry the onion in the margarine in a frying pan until tender. Add the beef and fry until brown, stirring frequently. Add the rice and fry for 1 minute, stirring frequently. Add the tomatoes and liquid and stir in the water. Add the salt and pepper and mix well. Cut the red peppers in large cubes and stir into the beef mixture. Cover. Bake at 350 degrees for 30 minutes or until rice is tender. 4 servings.

Beef-Farce Risotto (above)

RICE VERA CRUZ

1 lb. lean ground beef, crumbled	1/3 c. sherry
2 med. onions, chopped	2 tsp. chili powder
1 green pepper, chopped	Salt to taste
2 tbsp. oil or bacon drippings	1 c. sliced ripe olives
1 No. 303 can tomatoes	1 c. rice
1 can consomme	1 c. grated Cheddar cheese

Cook the beef, onions and green pepper in oil until brown, stirring frequently. Add the tomatoes, consomme, sherry, chili powder, salt and olives and bring to a boil. Stir in rice slowly and cook for several minutes. Pour into a 2-quart casserole and cover. Bake at 375 degrees for 30 minutes. Uncover and stir with a fork. Sprinkle cheese over top and bake for 15 minutes longer. Let stand for 5 to 10 minutes before serving. 6 servings.

Mrs. Jamie H. White, Signal Mountain, Tennessee

TEXAS HASH

3 lge. onions, thinly sliced	1/2 c. rice
1 lge. green pepper, minced	1 to 2 tsp. chili powder
3 tbsp. fat	2 tsp. salt
1 lb. ground beef, crumbled	1/8 tsp. pepper
2 c. cooked tomatoes	

Saute the onions and green pepper in fat in a skillet until tender. Add the beef and cook until brown. Stir in remaining ingredients. Pour into a greased 2-quart baking dish and cover. Bake at 350 degrees for 45 minutes. Remove cover and bake for 15 minutes longer. 6-8 servings.

Mrs. Ann Hoit, Arlington, Texas

CABBAGE-BEEF BAKE

1 2-lb. cabbage, shredded	1 tsp. salt
6 slices bacon	1/8 tsp. pepper
1/2 c. chopped onion	1 can spaghetti sauce with
1 c. rice	mushrooms
1 1/4 lb. ground beef, crumbled	1 c. water

Place half the cabbage in a greased large casserole. Saute the bacon in a frying pan until partially done. Remove from pan and drain. Stir onion and rice into bacon drippings in frying pan and cook over medium heat, stirring constantly, until rice is lightly browned. Spoon over cabbage in baking dish. Brown the ground beef in the frying pan. Spoon over rice mixture and sprinkle with salt and pepper. Top with remaining cabbage. Heat spaghetti sauce and water in the frying pan and pour over cabbage slowly. Add the bacon slices and cover with aluminum foil. Bake at 400 degrees for 50 minutes. Remove foil and bake for 10 minutes longer or until bacon is brown. 10 servings.

Mrs. R. M. Hays, Macon, Georgia

CHIP AND CHEESE CASSEROLE

6 slices bacon	4 slices Swiss cheese
3/4 lb. ground chuck	6 eggs, beaten
1/2 tsp. salt	1 1/2 c. milk
1/4 tsp. rosemary	4 tbsp. onion soup mix
Pepper	1/4 c. chopped parsley
4 oz. potato chips, crushed	

Fry the bacon in a skillet until crisp. Remove from skillet, drain and crumble. Cook the chuck in same skillet until partially done and drain. Add 1/4 teaspoon salt, rosemary and 1/4 teaspoon pepper. Place the potato chips in a 2-quart casserole and sprinkle with bacon. Cover with Swiss cheese and add the beef. Mix the eggs, milk, remaining salt, dash of pepper and onion soup mix and pour over beef. Sprinkle with parsley. Bake at 350 degrees for 20 minutes. Increase temperature to 375 degrees and bake for 5 minutes longer. 4 servings.

Mrs. Louis S. Harrison, Fort Royal, Virginia

EASY RAVIOLI FLORENTINE

2 10-oz. packages frozen chopped broccoli	1 lb. cottage cheese
1 15-oz. can spaghetti sauce with meat	2 15-oz. cans beef ravioli in sauce
	1/3 c. grated Parmesan cheese

Preheat oven to 350 degrees. Cook the broccoli according to package directions until tender. Drain and press out as much liquid as possible. Place in a greased large casserole. Spoon 1/2 can spaghetti sauce over the broccoli and spoon cottage cheese over the spaghetti sauce. Place ravioli in a single layer over the cottage cheese and spoon remaining spaghetti sauce over the ravioli. Sprinkle with Parmesan cheese. Bake for 40 to 45 minutes or until bubbly and serve hot. 6 servings.

Easy Ravioli Florentine (above)

pork

Pork is a favorite meat with southern homemakers who appreciate its versatility — and its highly adaptable flavor. It is no wonder that pork is so popular in casserole recipes. Creative southern cooks have found many new and exciting ways to serve pork.

In this section, you will find favorite recipes for casseroles featuring pork roast and chops, ham, bacon, and sausage. One appetite-pleasing recipe for Pineapple Pork combines pork shoulder, pineapple, and oriental herbs and spices into a tantalizingly different casserole. It's sure to bring compliments from your happy family and guests at a summer patio party. Another recipe is perfect for those crisp fall and winter dinners — Apple-Stuffed Pork Chops. Featuring a stuffing made with bread crumbs, apples, onion, and celery, this dish is a favorite.

You'll also be intrigued with the wide variety of ham casseroles featured. There's even a recipe for fondue, the recent arrival on the American cooking scene that is quickly becoming a real favorite. Ham and Cheese Fondue is perfect for a casual get-together or as a special party main dish.

As you browse through these pages, you'll find many more recipes just perfect for that spur-of-the-moment party . . . in-a-hurry dinner . . . for every occasion when you want to serve a hearty and palate-pleasing casserole.

PORK CHOPS-KRAUT AND BAKED APPLES

3 1/4 c. drained sauerkraut	1/4 c. melted butter
2 tsp. dried chopped chives	1/4 c. (firmly packed) brown
1/4 tsp. dillweed	sugar
6 loin pork chops, 1 in. thick	1/4 c. dark seedless raisins
Salt and pepper to taste	1 c. chicken broth or bouillon
3 tbsp. butter or margarine	1 1/2 tbsp. flour
6 med. red apples	1/2 c. heavy cream

Combine the sauerkraut, chives and dillweed and place in a large, shallow baking dish. Sprinkle the pork chops with salt and pepper and cook in the butter in a skillet until browned on both sides. Arrange on sauerkraut. Reserve 2 tablespoons pork drippings in skillet. Core the apples and pare 1 inch skin from top of each apple. Combine 2 tablespoons melted butter with brown sugar and raisins and stuff apples with the raisin mixture. Arrange apples at each end of baking dish and brush tops with remaining melted butter. Pour chicken broth over the chops and cover only the chops with aluminum foil. Bake in 350-degree oven for 1 hour, basting chops and apples with pan liquid. Remove foil from chops and bake for 20 minutes longer or until chops and apples are tender, basting occasionally. Drain off 1 cup broth and reserve. Heat the skillet with reserved drippings and stir in the flour. Add reserved broth and boil for 1 minute, stirring constantly. Stir in the cream and heat to serving temperature. Do not boil. Serve with pork chop mixture. 6 servings.

Photograph for this recipe on page 56.

PORK CHOPS WITH SOUR CHERRIES

4 thick loin pork chops	1 tbsp. sugar
Salt and pepper to taste	Grated peel of 1/2 lemon
1 c. rice	1/4 tsp. cinnamon
1 No. 2 can sour cherries	

Season the pork chops with salt and pepper and brown on both sides in a skillet. Place rice in a casserole. Drain the cherries and reserve juice. Mix the reserved juice with sugar, lemon peel and cinnamon. Place cherries over rice and pour juice mixture over cherries. Arrange pork chops on top and cover. Bake in 350-degree oven for 1 hour and 15 minutes. 4 servings.

Mrs. Joseph W. Fitzpatrick, Fort Knox, Kentucky

BAKED PORK CHOPS AND APPLES

4 pork chops, 1 in. thick	1 c. water
1 1/2 tsp. Kitchen Bouquet	1 tbsp. vinegar
1 tsp. salt	2 tbsp. brown sugar
1/8 tsp. pepper	1/2 c. seedless raisins
2 tbsp. flour	4 apples

Brush the pork chops with Kitchen Bouquet and brown in frying pan over moderate heat. Remove to a shallow baking dish and sprinkle with salt and pepper. Stir flour into fat in frying pan and add water, vinegar, sugar and raisins. Cook, stirring constantly, until thickened. Core the apples and cut into wedges. Arrange on pork chops and pour sauce over apples. Bake at 375 degrees for 45 minutes or until chops are tender, basting occasionally. Serve immediately. 4 servings.

Mrs. Robert C. Roylance, Clarksville, Tennessee

PORK CHOPS CREMORA

6 pork chops, 3/4 in. thick	1 1/2 lb. small potatoes
Salt and pepper to taste	1/3 c. white wine
1/2 tsp. dry mustard	2 tbsp. flour
5 tbsp. butter	1/2 c. light cream
1 beef bouillon cube	1/2 c. small stuffed olives
1 1/4 c. boiling water	

Trim excess fat from the pork chops. Mix salt, pepper and mustard and sprinkle over chops. Heat 3 tablespoons butter in a skillet. Add the chops and brown on both sides. Place in a casserole. Dissolve the bouillon cube in boiling water and pour over chops. Cover. Bake in 350-degree oven for 45 minutes or until chops are tender. Cook the potatoes in boiling water until tender. Drain and peel. Melt remaining butter in the skillet. Add the potatoes and cook over medium heat until crisp and brown. Sprinkle with salt and pepper and place in casserole with the chops. Add the wine to flour slowly, stirring constantly. Add the cream and stir into drippings in the skillet. Bring to a boil and cook for 1 minute, stirring constantly. Add the olives and pour over pork chop mixture. Bake until heated through. Garnish with cherries, if desired.

Pork Chops Cremora (above)

PINEAPPLE PORK

1 1/2 lb. boneless lean pork
   shoulder
1 tbsp. salad oil
1/2 c. chopped onion
1 1-lb. 4-oz. can pineapple
   chunks
1/4 c. (firmly packed) brown
   sugar

2 tbsp. cornstarch
1/2 tsp. salt
1/2 c. water
1/3 c. vinegar
2 tbsp. catsup
1 tbsp. soy sauce
1 lge. green pepper, cut
   in strips

Cut the pork in 1-inch cubes and brown in oil in a large skillet. Remove pork from skillet. Add onion to skillet and cook until soft. Add pork. Drain the pineapple and reserve syrup. Mix the brown sugar, cornstarch and salt in bowl and blend in water. Stir in reserved syrup, vinegar, catsup and soy sauce, then stir into pork mixture. Cook, stirring constantly, until thickened, then cook for 3 minutes. Pour into a casserole and cover casserole. Bake at 350 degrees for 1 hour or until pork is tender. Stir in green pepper and pineapple and cover. Bake for 3 minutes longer or until bubbly. Serve with Chinese noodles or hot rice. Yield: 4-6 servings.

Mrs. Thomas Downs, Hattiesburg, Mississippi

PORK CHOP-TOMATO CASSEROLE

6 pork chops
1 1/2 tsp. salt
1/4 tsp. pepper
Flour
1 tsp. shortening

2/3 c. chopped onions
1 clove of garlic, crushed
6 slices tomato, 1/2 in. thick
Sliced stuffed olives to taste

Season the pork chops with 1 teaspoon salt and 1/8 teaspoon pepper. Dredge with flour and brown in shortening in a skillet. Place in a shallow baking dish. Saute the onions and garlic in the skillet until brown and place half the mixture over chops. Sprinkle remaining salt and pepper on tomatoes and place 1 slice tomato on each pork chop. Dust lightly with flour. Place remaining onion mixture over tomato slices and cover. Bake at 375 degrees for 1 hour. Remove cover and bake for 15 minutes longer. Garnish with olives. 6 servings.

Mrs. Chester Curry, Ranson, West Virginia

PORK AND CORN ROAST

6 pork chops, 1/2 in. thick
1 tbsp. prepared mustard
1 No. 303 can golden
   cream-style corn
2/3 c. soft bread crumbs

2 tbsp. chopped onion
1 tbsp. chopped green pepper
1 tsp. salt
Dash of pepper
1 c. water

Spread the pork chops with mustard and brown in small amount of fat in a skillet. Combine the corn, crumbs, onion, green pepper, salt and pepper. Arrange chops in a baking dish. Drain fat from skillet and add water to skillet. Heat to boiling point and pour over chops. Top with corn mixture and cover. Bake at 350 degrees for 15 minutes. Uncover and bake for 45 minutes longer.

Mrs. Rex E. Steele, Bluefield, Virginia

LEMON-PORK WITH BRUSSELS SPROUTS

1/2 c. lemon juice	2 10-oz. packages frozen
2 c. bouillon	Brussels sprouts, thawed
2 tbsp. salad oil	2 tbsp. butter or margarine
1 tsp. salt	4 med. tomatoes, cut in wedges
1/2 tsp. pepper	2 1-lb. cans whole white
1 bouquet garni	potatoes
2 tbsp. minced onion	1/2 c. water
6 pork shoulder chops,	1/4 c. flour
1 in. thick	Parsley

Combine first 7 ingredients in a large bowl. Add the pork chops and Brussels sprouts and chill for 2 hours, turning pork chops occasionally. Remove pork chops and Brussels sprouts and reserve lemon mixture. Melt the butter in a skillet and brown pork chops on both sides. Add reserved lemon mixture and cover. Bake in 350-degree oven for 45 to 60 minutes or until tender. Add the Brussels sprouts and tomatoes. Drain the potatoes and slice. Add to pork chop mixture and cover. Bake for 20 minutes longer or until Brussels sprouts are tender. Remove the pork chops. Stir water into flour gradually and blend well. Add to the vegetable mixture and cook over low heat, stirring constantly, until thickened. Return pork chops to vegetable mixture and heat through. Garnish with parsley.

Lemon-Pork with Brussels Sprouts (above)

BAKED CHOPS AND CABBAGE

4 pork chops, 1/2 in. thick	1 1/2 tsp. salt
2 tbsp. fat	1/8 tsp. pepper
1/4 c. diced onion	3 med. potatoes, sliced
1 c. cream of celery soup	1 lb. cabbage, shredded
1/2 c. milk	1/4 c. flour

Brown the pork chops in hot fat in a heavy frypan and remove chops. Add the onion, soup, milk, salt and pepper to frypan and blend well. Place alternate layers of potatoes and cabbage in a 2-quart casserole, sprinkling each layer with flour. Pour soup mixture over top. Place chops over soup mixture and cover casserole. Bake at 350 degrees for 1 hour and 15 minutes. 4 servings.

Mrs. George Hemingway, Blairsville, Georgia

FRENCH CHOPS WITH CABBAGE

1 lge. green cabbage	4 tbsp. butter
Salt and pepper to taste	1/2 tsp. crumbled sage leaves
1 c. heavy cream	1/2 c. dry white wine
4 pork chops	1/4 c. grated Parmesan cheese

Wash, quarter, core and slice the cabbage and place in a saucepan. Sprinkle with salt and pepper and add cream. Bring to a boil, then simmer for 15 minutes. Trim excess fat from chops and saute chops in 2 tablespoons butter in a skillet until golden brown. Cover and cook over low heat until tender. Remove from skillet and sprinkle with salt and pepper. Add sage leaves and wine to skillet and scrape skillet to remove browned particles. Add to cabbage. Place half the cabbage mixture in shallow casserole and cover with chops. Add remaining cabbage mixture and sprinkle with cheese. Dot with remaining butter. Bake at 350 degrees for 45 minutes. 4 servings.

Mrs. Dan Firth, Baltimore, Maryland

PORK-VEGETABLE JUBILEE

1 lb. pork steak, cut in cubes	1 c. diced potatoes
Flour	Salt and pepper to taste
1 tbsp. shortening	1 c. water
1 c. peas	6 cloves
1 c. diced carrots	

Dredge the pork with flour and brown in shortening in a skillet. Remove pork from skillet and mix with the vegetables and seasonings. Place in a casserole. Add water to the drippings in skillet and bring to a boil. Pour over the pork mixture and add cloves. Bake at 350 degrees for 1 hour. 6 servings.

Mrs. Mae Caris, Pineview, Georgia

SWEET POTATO-PORK CHOP CASSEROLE

6 pork chops
1 tsp. salt
1/8 tsp. pepper
4 med. sweet potatoes, sliced

1 med. onion, chopped
1 c. water
1 tsp. Worcestershire sauce

Brown the pork chops in small amount of fat in a skillet. Place in a large casserole and sprinkle with half the salt and pepper. Place sweet potatoes over chops and sprinkle with remaining salt and pepper. Saute onion in the skillet. Add the water and Worcestershire sauce and mix well. Pour over potatoes and cover. Bake at 375 degrees for 1 hour and 30 minutes. 6 servings.

Martha Wood, Grenada, Mississippi

FRESH VEGETABLES AND PORK ORIENTAL

1/2 lb. fresh mushrooms
1/4 c. butter or margarine
4 c. diagonally sliced celery
1 med. green pepper, sliced
1 med. red pepper, sliced
1 med. onion, sliced
2 c. cubed cooked pork

1 can beef broth
1 tbsp. cornstarch
3 tbsp. soy sauce
1/2 tsp. salt
1/2 tsp. ground ginger
1/8 tsp. ground pepper

Rinse, pat dry and halve the mushrooms and set aside. Melt the butter in a medium skillet. Add the celery and saute for 5 minutes. Add the mushrooms, green and red peppers and onion and saute for 5 minutes longer. Add the pork and broth and bring to a boil. Cover. Bake at 350 degrees for about 15 minutes and uncover. Blend the cornstarch with soy sauce, salt, ginger and pepper and stir into pork mixture. Bake for 10 minutes longer or until thickened. Serve with rice, if desired. 6 servings.

Fresh Vegetables and Pork Oriental (above)

TENDERLOIN WITH MACARONI

1 1/2 c. macaroni	1 tsp. salt
4 tbsp. chopped onion	Dash of pepper
2 tbsp. butter	2 c. canned tomatoes
2 c. cubed cooked pork	3/4 c. grated cheese
tenderloin	3 fried sausage patties

Cook the macaroni according to package directions and drain. Saute onion in butter in a saucepan until brown. Add the pork tenderloin, salt and pepper and cook until pork is browned. Add the macaroni and tomatoes and pour into a baking dish. Sprinkle with cheese and crumble sausage over top. Bake at 350 degrees until cheese is melted. 8 servings.

Mrs. W. F. Meadows, Iron Gate, Virginia

PORK-ONION CASSEROLE

2 lb. ground pork shoulder	1 can tomato soup
1/2 lb. wide egg noodles	1 tsp. salt
1 lge. Spanish onion, chopped	1/2 lb. grated sharp cheese

Mix all ingredients and turn into a greased 3-quart casserole. Cover. Bake at 375 degrees for 1 hour. 8 servings.

Mrs. A. D. Schaaf, Norfolk, Virginia

TENDERLOIN-NOODLE CASSEROLE

6 oz. noodles	3 tbsp. flour
6 slices pork tenderloin,	1 c. milk
1/2 in. thick	3/4 c. crumbled bleu cheese
1 1/4 tsp. salt	3 tbsp. chopped green pepper
Pepper to taste	3 tbsp. chopped pimento
3 tbsp. butter	

Cook the noodles in boiling, salted water until tender, then rinse and drain. Brown pork tenderloin on both sides in small amount of hot fat in a skillet and season with 1/2 teaspoon salt and pepper. Melt the butter in a saucepan and blend in flour, remaining salt and pepper. Stir in milk and cook, stirring, until thick. Add the cheese and stir until cheese melts. Stir in the green pepper and pimento. Place alternate layers of noodles, cheese sauce and pork in a 10 x 6 x 1 1/2-inch baking dish. Bake at 350 degrees for 30 minutes. 6 servings.

Mrs. Louis W. Talley, Leesville, Louisiana

PORK STEAK AND NOODLE CASSEROLE

2 lb. pork steak, cut in cubes	1 c. diced celery
2 tbsp. margarine	1 8-oz. package thin noodles
1 sm. onion, diced	2 tsp. seasoned salt

Dash of pepper	1 c. grated sharp Italian
1 can mushroom soup	cheese
1 soup can water	3 tbsp. dry bread crumbs

Brown the pork in 1 tablespoon margarine in a skillet. Add a small amount of water and simmer until partially done. Cook the onion and celery in a small amount of water until partially done and drain. Cook the noodles according to package directions, then rinse and drain. Combine the pork, onion mixture, noodles, seasonings, soup and 1 soup can water and pour into a large greased casserole. Cover with cheese and crumbs and dot with remaining margarine. Bake, covered, at 350 degrees for 1 hour. Uncover and bake for 15 minutes longer. 8 servings.

Mrs. Alva Butler, Reydon, Oklahoma

AUTUMN CASSEROLE

1 c. diced celery	6 rib pork chops
1 med. onion, chopped	1 can okra
1 clove of garlic, minced	1 c. rice
1 can tomato soup	1 can red kidney beans
1 c. water	3/4 c. sliced ripe olives
1 tsp. salt	1 can whole kernel corn
1 bay leaf, crumbled	

Saute the celery, onion and garlic in small amount of fat in a saucepan until tender. Stir in the soup, water and seasonings and heat to boiling point. Brown the pork chops in a large frying pan and set aside. Combine the okra, rice, beans, olives and corn. Add to celery mixture and mix well. Place in a 2-quart baking dish and place pork chops on top in shape of pinwheel. Cover. Bake at 350 degrees for 1 hour or until chops are well done. 6-8 servings.

Mrs. Edwin I. Croom, Columbus, Georgia

ORIENTAL PORK CHOPS

1 c. rice	2 tbsp. shortening
Salt	2 tbsp. lemon juice
1 can onion soup	1 11-oz. can mandarin
1 tsp. thyme	oranges
4 to 6 pork chops	3/4 c. pitted cooked prunes
Pepper to taste	

Mix the rice with 1 teaspoon salt, soup, 1/2 cup water and thyme in a shallow baking dish. Season the pork chops with salt to taste and pepper and brown in the shortening in a skillet. Place on rice mixture and sprinkle with lemon juice. Cover. Bake at 350 degrees for 30 minutes. Drain the mandarin oranges and reserve syrup. Place prunes and orange segments on chops and pour reserved syrup over all. Cover and bake for 20 minutes longer.

Mrs. Claude Parks, Whitney, Texas

ITALIAN CHOPS WITH RICE

4 pork chops	1/4 tsp. Worcestershire sauce
Salt and pepper to taste	1 1/4 c. tomato juice
1 tsp. oregano	1 c. boiling water
2 tbsp. shortening	3/4 c. rice
3 tbsp. onion soup mix	

Season the pork chops with salt, pepper and oregano and brown in hot shortening in a skillet. Place in a greased 1 1/2-quart casserole. Combine remaining ingredients and pour over chops. Cover. Bake at 350 degrees for 40 to 45 minutes. 4 servings.

Mrs. Orville Kennedy, Alexandria, Louisiana

BROWN RICE AND PORK CHOPS

4 pork chops	1 1/2 c. water
3 tbsp. shortening	1/4 tsp. pepper
3 tsp. salt	1/4 c. chopped green pepper
1 c. rice	1/2 c. chopped onion
1 bouillon cube	

Brown the pork chops in shortening in a skillet and remove from skillet. Season with 1 teaspoon salt. Add the rice to drippings in skillet and brown lightly, stirring constantly. Dissolve the bouillon cube in water and stir into rice. Add the pepper, green pepper, onion and remaining salt and pour into a casserole. Place chops on rice mixture and cover. Bake at 350 degrees for 1 hour. 4 servings.

Mrs. John Farmer, Columbia, South Carolina

SPARERIB-BEAN BAKE

4 lb. spareribs	Ground ginger
1 13 1/2-oz. can pineapple	1 tbsp. Worcestershire sauce
chunks	1/2 tsp. onion salt
2 tbsp. brown sugar	3 16-oz. cans pork
1 1/2 tsp. salt	and beans
Ground cloves	

Cut the spareribs in 2-rib pieces and place in 13 x 9-inch baking dish. Drain the pineapple and reserve syrup. Mix the brown sugar, salt, 1/4 teaspoon cloves, 1/4 teaspoon ginger, Worcestershire sauce and reserved syrup and brush half the mixture on spareribs. Sprinkle spareribs with onion salt. Bake at 350 degrees for 1 hour, basting with drippings every 15 minutes. Remove spareribs from baking dish and set aside. Pour off drippings from baking dish. Combine the pork and beans, pineapple chunks, 1/8 teaspoon cloves and 1/8 teaspoon ginger in the baking dish and arrange spareribs on bean mixture. Spoon remaining brown sugar mixture over spareribs. Bake for 1 hour longer or until beans mixture is heated through. 6 servings.

Mrs. Browning Graham, Morgan City, Louisiana

BAKED PORK CHOPS AND STUFFING

4 pork chops	1/4 c. water
3 c. soft bread crumbs	Pepper to taste
2 tbsp. chopped onion	1 can cream of mushroom soup
1/4 c. melted butter or	1/3 c. water
margarine	

Brown the pork chops on both sides in a skillet and place in a shallow baking dish. Mix the bread crumbs, onion, butter, 1/4 cup water and pepper and place on pork chops. Blend the soup and 1/3 cup water and pour over all. Bake at 350 degrees for 1 hour or until pork is tender. 4 servings.

Mrs. Dale McLemore, Roxie, Mississippi

PORK CHOPS WITH DRESSING

4 slices bread	1/8 tsp. thyme
1 sm. onion, chopped	1/2 c. water
1 stalk celery, chopped	4 pork chops
1/4 c. butter	1 tbsp. shortening
1/8 tsp. savory	1/4 tsp. paprika
1/2 tsp. salt	

Cut the bread in cubes and toast until golden brown. Saute the onion and celery in butter in a saucepan until tender and add the savory, salt, thyme and water. Mix with bread cubes and pour into a 2-quart casserole. Brown the pork chops in shortening in a skillet and place on dressing. Sprinkle with paprika and cover. Bake at 350 degrees for 45 minutes. Remove cover and bake for 10 minutes longer. 4 servings.

Mrs. Bennie Ricks, Moultrie, Georgia

APPLE-STUFFED PORK CHOPS

6 lge. pork chops	1 tsp. salt
1 c. chopped apples	1/2 tsp. pepper
1 1/2 c. bread crumbs	1 tbsp. sugar
1/4 c. chopped onion	2 to 3 tbsp. milk
1/4 c. chopped celery	

Cut through lean portion of each pork chop to form a pocket. Combine the apples, bread crumbs, onion, celery, salt, pepper and sugar and add enough milk to moisten. Stuff into pockets in chops. Place chops in a shallow baking pan. Bake at 350 degrees for 1 hour, basting occasionally with drippings. Cover and bake for 30 minutes longer. 6 servings.

Mrs. Warner Lowe, Carlisle, Kentucky

COUNTRY CASSEROLE

1 6-oz. can mushroom crowns	2 tsp. Worcestershire sauce
3 c. diced cooked ham	5 drops of hot sauce
6 hard-cooked eggs, sliced	3/4 c. dry bread crumbs
1 can cream of celery soup	3 tbsp. melted butter or
1/2 c. milk	margarine
2 c. grated American cheese	

Drain the mushrooms. Place alternate layers of ham, eggs and mushrooms in a 2-quart casserole. Combine the soup, milk, cheese, Worcestershire sauce and hot sauce in a saucepan and heat, stirring, until cheese melts. Pour over casserole. Mix the crumbs and butter and sprinkle over top. Bake at 375 degrees for 25 minutes. 6 servings.

Mrs. Bobbye Wooleyhan, Sudlersville, Maryland

BAKED DEVILED EGGS AND HAM

10 hard-cooked eggs	10 slices boiled ham
1/4 c. minced parsley	2 tbsp. finely chopped onion
1 tbsp. prepared mustard	1 tbsp. chopped pimentos
1/4 c. mayonnaise	1/8 tsp. dillweed
2 tsp. vinegar	1 can cream of mushroom soup
1/2 tsp. seasoned salt	2/3 c. evaporated milk

Cut the eggs in half and remove yolks. Place the egg yolks in a bowl and mash. Add 2 tablespoons parsley, mustard, mayonnaise, vinegar and seasoned salt and mix well. Fill egg whites with yolk mixture and place 2 halves together. Place each egg diagonally on 1 ham slice. Fold ham around egg and secure with toothpicks. Place in a 12 x 7 1/2 x 2-inch baking dish. Combine remaining parsley and remaining ingredients and pour over eggs. Bake at 350 degrees for 20 to 25 minutes and garnish with additional parsley. 8-10 servings.

Mrs. Bill Stout, Piedmont, Oklahoma

HAM SOUFFLE

16 slices sandwich bread	1/2 tsp. mustard
8 slices sharp cheese	1 tsp. seasoned salt
2 c. ground cooked ham	1/2 c. melted butter
6 eggs, well beaten	2 c. crushed corn flakes
3 c. milk	

Cut crusts from the bread and place 8 slices in a large, shallow baking pan. Cover with slices of cheese and spread with ham. Mix the eggs, milk, mustard and salt. Place remaining bread on ham and pour milk mixture over bread. Refrigerate overnight. Mix the butter and corn flake crumbs and sprinkle on top. Bake at 350 degrees for 1 hour and 30 minutes. Serve with mushroom sauce, if desired. 8 servings.

Mrs. Charles William Nipson, West Palm Beach, Florida

HAM SANDWICH CASSEROLE

12 slices bread	3 1/2 c. milk
1/2 lb. sliced Swiss cheese	1/2 tsp. salt
Mustard	1 can mushroom soup
1/2 lb. ground ham	2 hard-cooked eggs, chopped
Butter or margarine	Chopped pimento to taste
4 eggs, slightly beaten	

Cut the crusts from bread and place 6 slices bread in a large, shallow pan. Cover with cheese and spread with thin layer of mustard. Cover with ham. Butter remaining bread and place on ham, buttered side up. Mix the beaten eggs, 3 cups milk and salt in a bowl and pour over sandwiches. Refrigerate for several hours. Bake at 300 degrees for 1 hour. Mix the mushroom soup with remaining milk in a saucepan and heat through. Add the hard-cooked eggs and pimento and serve with ham mixture. 6 servings.

Mrs. W. H. Patterson, Fort Stewart, Georgia

HAM AND CHEESE FONDUE

6 slices bread	3 eggs, slightly beaten
3 tbsp. butter or margarine	2 c. milk
6 slices Cheddar cheese	1 tsp. salt
3 slices boiled ham	1/4 tsp. pepper
1 tbsp. prepared mustard	

Spread 3 slices bread with butter and top each with 1 slice cheese. Place 1 slice ham over each slice cheese and add remaining cheese. Spread remaining bread slices with mustard and place on cheese to make sandwiches. Cut each sandwich into nine cubes and place in a well-greased 2-quart casserole. Mix the eggs, milk, salt and pepper and pour over bread cubes. Place casserole in pan of hot water. Bake at 350 degrees for 1 hour or until a knife inserted in center comes out clean. 6 servings.

Mrs. Walter Dilworth, Booneville, Mississippi

DIXIE CASSEROLE

4 tbsp. butter or margarine	6 hard-cooked eggs, sliced
4 tbsp. flour	1/2 lb. sliced boiled ham
2 c. milk	1 1/2 c. cooked whole kernel
1 tsp. salt	corn
Dash of pepper	1 c. soft bread crumbs

Melt the butter in top of a double boiler and stir in flour. Add the milk gradually and cook over boiling water, stirring constantly, until thick. Add the salt and pepper and cook for 5 minutes longer, stirring frequently. Place half the eggs in a casserole and add half the ham. Add half the corn and cover with half the white sauce. Repeat layers. Top with the bread crumbs and dot with additional butter. Bake at 400 degrees for 15 minutes.

Mrs. Alberta E. Veith, Louisville, Kentucky

HAM AND CHEESE CASSEROLE

4 eggs, separated	1 tsp. salt
1 c. ground cooked ham	1/2 tsp. Worcestershire sauce
1 c. cubed American cheese	1 1/2 c. macaroni
1 tbsp. chopped parsley	1 c. milk
1 tsp. onion juice	1/2 c. grated cheese

Mix the egg yolks with ham, cubed cheese and seasonings in a bowl. Cook the macaroni according to package directions and stir into the ham mixture. Fold in stiffly beaten egg whites and place in a greased 2-quart baking dish. Pour milk over top and sprinkle with grated cheese. Bake at 350 degrees for 40 to 45 minutes. 6 servings.

Mrs. Jack Mullikin, Tollesboro, Kentucky

GOLDEN CASSEROLE

2 c. cooked macaroni	1/2 c. cooked sliced mushrooms
1 c. cubed cooked ham	1 1/2 c. medium cheese sauce
1 1/2 c. cooked green peas	Buttered crumbs

Mix first 4 ingredients in a bowl. Add the cheese sauce and mix. Pour into a casserole and cover with buttered crumbs. Bake at 350 degrees for 45 minutes. 6 servings.

Mrs. J. L. Hybart, Hybart, Alabama

MEXICAN TAMALIO

2 med. green peppers, diced	1/4 c. butter or margarine
1 8-oz. package elbow	1 glass Cheddar process cheese
macaroni	1/2 c. flour
1/2 lb. sliced ham	3 c. milk

Place the green peppers in a saucepan and cover with water. Bring to a boil, then simmer for 15 minutes. Drain and set aside. Cook the macaroni according to package directions. Drain and set aside. Fry the ham in a skillet until brown. Melt the butter and cheese in a double boiler and stir in flour all at once. Stir in milk slowly and cook until thick, stirring constantly. Place the macaroni, green peppers and ham in alternate layers in a greased baking dish and pour cheese sauce over top. Bake at 350 degrees for 35 minutes or until browned. 4-6 servings.

Mrs. John F. McCloskey, Sanford, Florida

SMOKED HAM FINESSE

8 oz. egg noodles	1 1/2 c. milk
2 c. ground smoked ham	Salt and pepper to taste
2 eggs, well beaten	Butter

Cook the noodles according to package directions and drain. Place alternate layers of noodles and ham in a 9-inch baking dish. Mix the eggs, milk, salt and pepper and pour over ham mixture. Dot with butter. Bake in 350-degree oven for 45 minutes. 6 servings.

Mrs. Jewell Payne, Apple Springs, Texas

HAM AND NOODLE CASSEROLE

3/4 c. diced onions	1 1/2 c. diced ham
1/2 c. diced green pepper	1 tsp. salt
2 tsp. salad oil	1/4 tsp. pepper
1/2 lb. broad noodles	1/2 tsp. paprika
1 3/4 c. canned tomatoes	1/2 lb. Cheddar cheese, grated
1 c. water	

Cook the onions and green pepper in oil in a saucepan over low heat until transparent. Add the noodles, tomatoes, water, ham, salt, pepper and paprika and simmer for 10 minutes. Stir in the cheese and turn into a greased 2-quart casserole. Bake in 350-degree oven for 40 to 45 minutes.

Mrs. Frank J. Lesslie, Decatur, Georgia

GOURMET HAM AND CHEESE CASSEROLE

1 c. milk	1/2 c. diced celery
1 8-oz. package cream cheese	1/2 c. chopped green pepper
1/2 tsp. salt	1/2 c. grated Parmesan cheese
1/2 tsp. garlic salt	1 4-oz. package noodles
1 1/2 c. diced boiled ham	

Add milk to cream cheese gradually, blending until smooth. Add remaining ingredients except 1/2 cup Parmesan cheese and noodles and mix well. Cook the noodles according to package directions and mix with ham mixture. Place in a 1 1/2-quart casserole and sprinkle with remaining Parmesan cheese. Bake at 350 degrees for 25 to 30 minutes. 10 servings.

Mrs. J. W. Nickolson, Lawrenceville, Georgia

HAM AND RICE CASSEROLE

2 c. chopped cooked ham	1 egg, slightly beaten
1 tsp. salt	1 c. milk
1/4 tsp. pepper	4 c. cooked rice

Season the ham with salt and pepper. Mix the egg with milk. Place half the rice in a greased casserole and spread half the ham mixture over rice. Cover with half the egg mixture and repeat layers. Bake in 375-degree oven for 30 to 40 minutes. 8 servings.

Mrs. Guy Bussard, Deerfield, Virginia

HAM LUNCHEON PIE

2 c. crushed crackers	1 c. milk
1/3 c. soft margarine	3 eggs, beaten
1 lb. ground ham	2 tbsp. chopped green pepper
1 med. onion, chopped	1/2 lb. cheese, grated
1 c. cooked rice	

Mix the cracker crumbs with margarine and reserve 2/3 cup for topping. Press remaining crumb mixture in a baking dish. Combine the ham, onion and rice and place over crumb mixture in baking dish. Mix the milk and eggs and stir in green pepper and cheese. Pour over the ham mixture and sprinkle with reserved crumb mixture. Bake at 350 degrees for 45 minutes. 6 servings.

Nancy Simonton, Greenville, South Carolina

SAFFRON RICE WITH HAM

1 c. saffron rice	1 3-oz. can sliced
2 1/2 c. boiling water	mushrooms
1 tsp. salt	1/2 c. slivered almonds
1 1/2 c. cubed smoked ham	1/2 c. sliced ripe olives
1/4 c. butter	

Pour the rice into water in a saucepan and add salt. Boil for 1 minute. Cover tightly and reduce heat. Simmer for 20 minutes, stirring once, then drain. Saute ham and mushrooms in butter in a saucepan until brown. Add the rice, almonds and olives. Pour into a shallow baking dish and cover. Bake in 350-degree oven for 15 minutes. 6 servings.

Mrs. Joseph Costello, Prattville, Alabama

RICE AND HAM CREOLE

1 onion, chopped	2 c. cooked tomatoes
1 slice cooked ham, chopped	1/8 tsp. salt
1 tbsp. butter	Paprika to taste
1 c. cooked rice	Bread crumbs

Combine the onion, ham, butter, rice and tomatoes in a bowl and season with salt and paprika. Mix thoroughly. Place in a baking dish and cover with bread crumbs. Bake at 400 degrees for 15 minutes.

Mrs. Jake Thomas, Manchester, Kentucky

GREEN BEANS AND HAM·

1 c. cubed cooked ham	Salt and pepper to taste
1 c. cooked diced potatoes	3/4 c. thin white sauce
1 c. cooked chopped green	Buttered bread crumbs
beans	

Place alternate layers of ham, potatoes and beans in a casserole and season with salt and pepper. Add the white sauce and cover with buttered crumbs. Bake at 375 degrees for 25 to 30 minutes. 6 servings.

Mrs. H. R. Perdue, Natchez, Mississippi

BAKED BEANS AND HAM CASSEROLE

1 med. onion, chopped	**1/2 c. water**
1/4 c. chopped green pepper	**1 tbsp. wine vinegar**
1 c. cooked ham, cut in strips	**1/2 tsp. salt**
2 tbsp. butter or margarine	**1 1-lb. can baked beans**
1/2 c. tomato paste	**4 slices bacon**

Saute the onion, green pepper and ham in butter in a saucepan until onion is tender. Add the tomato paste, water, vinegar and salt and simmer for about 5 minutes. Add the beans and turn into a 1-quart casserole. Place the bacon on top. Bake at 350 degrees for 30 minutes or until bubbly and browned. 4-6 servings.

Mrs. Carol Ann Young, Swannanoa, North Carolina

HAM AND ARTICHOKE MEDLEY

1 9-oz. package frozen artichokes	**2 tbsp. minced scallions**
1/2 bay leaf	**1/8 tsp. pepper**
2 10 1/2-oz. cans cream of chicken soup	**2 c. diced cooked ham**
	1 1/2 c. cooked rice
1/2 c. dry white wine	**4 hard-cooked eggs, sliced**

Cook the artichokes according to package directions, adding bay leaf to water. Drain and remove bay leaf. Mix the soup, wine, scallions and pepper in a bowl. Stir in the ham, artichokes, rice and eggs and mix gently but thoroughly. Turn into a 2-quart casserole. Bake at 375 degrees for 35 minutes. 6 servings.

Ham and Artichoke Medley (above)

Yam and Ham-Cranberry Casserole (below)

YAM AND HAM-CRANBERRY CASSEROLE

1 med. unpeeled orange	6 med. cooked yams, sliced
1 tbsp. butter or margarine	1 1/2 lb. cubed cooked ham
1/2 c. whole cranberry sauce	1/2 c. chopped pecans
1/2 c. maple-blended syrup	1 tbsp. brown sugar

Quarter the orange and grind. Melt the butter in a saucepan and stir in the orange, cranberry sauce and syrup. Simmer for 5 minutes or until blended. Place 1/2 of the yams in a 2-quart casserole and add 1/2 of the ham. Pour 1/2 of the cranberry mixture over ham. Add remaining yams, then add remaining ham. Add the pecans to remaining cranberry mixture and pour over ham. Sprinkle with brown sugar. Bake in 350-degree oven for 30 minutes. 6-8 servings.

GYPSY CASSEROLE

1 1 1/2-in. slice smoked ham	4 turnips, halved
4 potatoes, halved	1/2 c. light molasses
6 carrots, halved	1 c. milk
4 sm. onions, halved	1/2 tsp. paprika

Place the ham in a greased large casserole and arrange vegetables over ham. Combine the molasses, milk and paprika and pour over vegetables. Cover. Bake at 350 degrees for 1 hour and 30 minutes. Uncover and bake for 30 minutes longer. 8 servings.

Mrs. Zadie Harvey, Pelahatchie, Mississippi

HAWAIIAN HAM

1 No. 303 can sliced pineapple	3 cooked sweet potatoes,
2 slices ham, 1 in. thick	halved
Prepared mustard	1/4 c. brown sugar

Drain the pineapple and reserve syrup. Cut each ham slice into 3 pieces and spread with mustard. Place in a greased shallow baking dish. Top each piece of ham with 1 pineapple slice and half a potato. Pour reserved pineapple syrup over top and sprinkle with brown sugar. Bake at 325 degrees for 1 hour. 6 servings.

Mrs. W. R. Atwood, Shelbyville, Tennessee

HAM STEAK AND YAMS

1/4 c. diced candied orange peel	1 tbsp. lemon juice
1/2 c. honey	1 ham steak, 1/2 in. thick
1/2 c. orange juice	1 1-lb. can yams, drained

Combine the orange peel, honey, orange juice and lemon juice in a bowl and mix well. Cut the ham in serving pieces and place in a casserole. Place the yams over ham and pour the honey mixture over yams. Bake at 350 degrees for 30 minutes.

Mrs. John Clicque, Union City, Tennessee

HOMINY CASSEROLE

1 1/2 lb. sliced bacon	1 c. canned tomatoes
1 No. 2 can hominy, drained	Salt and pepper to taste
1 med. onion, chopped	1 tsp. chili powder
1 tbsp. flour	1/4 lb. mild cheese, grated

Fry the bacon in a skillet until crisp. Remove from skillet and crumble. Drain all except 1/2 cup bacon fat from skillet. Fry the hominy and onion in fat in skillet until lightly browned. Add the flour and stir well. Add the tomatoes and seasonings and cook over medium heat for about 15 minutes. Remove from heat and add bacon. Pour into a greased casserole and sprinkle with cheese. Bake at 350 degrees for 30 minutes. 6 servings.

Mrs. T. C. Holland, Huntsville, Alabama

BACON-SOUR CREAM CASSEROLE

1/2 lb. sliced bacon	1/2 tsp. onion salt
1 c. macaroni	1 tsp. Worcestershire sauce
1 c. grated American process cheese	1 tbsp. chopped pimento
1/2 c. sour cream	2 tbsp. chopped green pepper
1/4 c. milk	1 2-oz. can mushroom stems and pieces
1/4 tsp. salt	Dash of pepper

Cook the bacon in a skillet over low heat until crisp, then drain and crumble. Cook the macaroni according to package directions. Add the bacon and remaining ingredients and mix well. Place in a 1-quart casserole. Bake at 350 degrees for 30 minutes. 4 servings.

Mrs. Henre Plante, New Orleans, Louisiana

SAUSAGE-CORN BREAD CASSEROLE

1 lb. bulk pork sausage	1 c. yellow cornmeal
1 c. sifted flour	2 eggs
1/4 c. sugar	1 c. milk
4 tsp. baking powder	1/4 c. soft shortening
3/4 tsp. salt	2 tbsp. chopped green pepper

Crumble the sausage and brown in a skillet. Drain and reserve 3 tablespoons drippings for gravy. Place sausage in a 9-inch square pan. Sift the flour, sugar, baking powder and salt together into a bowl and stir in cornmeal. Add the eggs, milk, shortening and green pepper and stir just until mixed. Pour over sausage. Bake at 425 degrees for 20 to 25 minutes.

Onion Gravy

3 tbsp. chopped onion	2 c. milk
4 tbsp. flour	1/2 tsp. Worcestershire sauce
Salt and pepper to taste	

Cook the onion in reserved drippings in a saucepan and blend in the flour, salt and pepper. Add the milk and cook until thick, stirring constantly. Stir in Worcestershire sauce and serve with sausage mixture.

Mrs. C. M. Mize, Lakeland, Florida

SAUSAGE CASSEROLE

1/2 tsp. salt	1 c. milk
2 c. boiling water	1/4 c. grated cheese
1 c. grits	4 eggs, beaten
1/2 stick butter or margarine	1/2 c. bulk pork sausage

Add the salt to water in a saucepan. Stir in grits slowly and cook until thick, stirring frequently. Add the butter, milk and cheese and mix well. Add the eggs slowly, stirring constantly. Crumble the sausage and stir into grits mixture. Pour into a greased casserole. Bake at 350 degrees for 30 minutes. 4-6 servings.

Mrs. Jessie Lester, Alexandria, Virginia

BRIDGE NIGHT CASSEROLE

1 lb. pork sausage links	1/4 tsp. nutmeg
3 c. cooked noodles	1/4 tsp. cinnamon
1 c. applesauce	1/2 c. grated cheese
2 tsp. lemon juice	

Place the sausage in a shallow pan. Bake at 400 degrees for 25 minutes, turning once. Drain and reserve drippings. Place half the noodles in a casserole and drizzle with 4 tablespoons reserved drippings. Add applesauce, lemon juice and spices, then add remaining noodles. Place sausages on top and sprinkle with cheese. Bake at 350 degrees for 10 minutes.

Kathryn S. Johnson, St. Petersburg, Florida

SPAGHETTI-SAUSAGE CASSEROLE

1/2 lb. sausage links	1/4 tsp. salt
6 oz. spaghetti	Dash of pepper
2 hard-cooked eggs	1 can mushroom soup
1 tbsp. salad dressing	1/2 c. milk
1/2 tsp. prepared mustard	

Brown the sausage in a heavy skillet. Cook spaghetti according to package directions. Drain and rinse. Cut eggs in half. Press egg yolks through a sieve and add the salad dressing, mustard, salt and pepper. Fill egg whites. Combine the soup and milk and stir until smooth. Fold in spaghetti and pour into a greased 1 1/2-quart casserole. Arrange sausage and eggs on top. Bake at 350 degrees for 20 minutes. 4-6 servings.

Mrs. Jack Mollenbour, Sharon, Tennessee

CURRIED EGG NOODLES WITH SAUSAGE

Salt	1/2 tsp. curry powder
4 to 6 qt. boiling water	1/4 tsp. pepper
1 lb. medium egg noodles	2 lb. link sausage
1/2 c. butter or margarine	3 c. applesauce
1/2 c. flour	Cinnamon
1 qt. milk	

Add 2 tablespoons salt to boiling water and add noodles gradually so that water continues to boil. Cook, stirring occasionally, until tender and drain in a colander. Melt the butter in a saucepan and blend in flour. Add milk gradually and cook over medium heat, stirring constantly, until thickened. Add the noodles, curry powder, 2 teaspoons salt and pepper. Cook the sausage in a skillet until browned and drain on absorbent paper. Place half the noodle mixture in a 3-quart shallow baking dish and top with half the sausage. Repeat layers and top with applesauce. Sprinkle cinnamon lightly over applesauce. Bake in 375-degree oven for 20 to 25 minutes. 8 servings.

Curried Egg Noodles with Sausage (above)

Quick and Easy Casserole (below)

QUICK AND EASY CASSEROLE

1 8-oz. package brown-and- serve sausages 1 c. pitted prunes	1 15-oz. package chicken-rice mix

Brown the sausages according to package directions, adding prunes after the sausages are partially cooked. Prepare the chicken-rice mix according to package directions and place in a 1-quart casserole. Arrange the sausages and prunes on top and cover. Bake at 325 degrees for 15 minutes. 4 servings.

AMARILLO SAUSAGE BAKE

1 lb. bulk sausage 3/4 c. rice 1 can chicken gumbo soup	1 c. water Salt and pepper to taste 1/4 tsp. oregano

Crumble the sausage and brown well in a heavy frying pan. Drain off fat. Mix in remaining ingredients and pour into a casserole. Cover. Bake at 350 degrees for 35 to 45 minutes. 3-4 servings.

Mrs. Donald Tryk, North Palm Beach, Florida

SPANISH RICE WITH SAUSAGE

6 strips bacon, diced 15 sm. sausage links, sliced 1 green pepper, diced 1 lge. onion, chopped	2 tbsp. flour 1 1/2 c. tomato sauce Salt and pepper to taste 2 c. rice

Fry the bacon and sausage in a skillet until brown and remove from skillet. Saute the green pepper and onion in drippings in the skillet until soft. Add the flour and stir well. Add tomato sauce and seasonings. Cook the rice according to package directions and stir into onion mixture. Place in a casserole and top with sausage mixture. Bake at 350 degrees for 10 minutes. 6 servings.

Mrs. Elden Brunet, Oakdale, Louisiana

CORN AND SAUSAGE CASSEROLE

3/4 lb. bulk sausage	1 c. cream-style corn
1 egg, beaten	1 sm. green pepper, chopped
1 c. cracker crumbs	1 can tomato sauce
1 1/4 c. milk, heated	

Cook the sausage in a skillet until partially done. Add the egg, crumbs, 1 cup milk, corn and green pepper and mix well. Pour into a greased casserole. Mix the tomato sauce and remaining milk and pour over sausage mixture. Bake at 350 degrees for 1 hour. Top with cheese, if desired.

Mrs. Hubert Garrett, Bolivar, Tennessee

BAKED BEAN AND SAUSAGE CASSEROLE

1 lb. sausage	1 can baked beans
3 med. apples, sliced	

Fry the sausage in a skillet until partially done and pour off excess fat. Place sausage in a casserole and cover with apples. Top with baked beans. Bake at 350 degrees for 1 hour. 4 servings.

Mildred Smith, St. Petersburg, Florida

SOUTHERN SAUSAGE CASSEROLE

1/2 lb. bulk pork sausage	1 c. cooked kidney beans
1 c. chopped celery	1 c. sifted flour
1/4 c. chopped onion	1 1/2 tsp. baking powder
1/4 c. chopped green pepper	2 tbsp. shortening
2 tbsp. minced parsley	1/2 c. shredded American
3/4 tsp. salt	cheese
3/4 c. tomato paste	1/2 c. milk
3/4 c. water	

Brown the sausage in a heavy skillet. Add the celery, onion, green pepper and parsley and brown lightly. Drain off excess fat and season with 1/4 teaspoon salt. Combine the tomato paste and water and add to sausage mixture. Add the beans and mix well. Cover. Simmer for 10 minutes and pour into a 1 1/2-quart casserole. Sift the flour with baking powder and remaining salt into a bowl and cut in shortening until mixture is consistency of crumbs. Add the cheese and milk and mix just until flour is moistened. Drop by spoonfuls over sausage mixture. Bake at 425 degrees for 20 minutes. 6 servings.

Mrs. James Elms, Jamestown, Arkansas

poultry

An old saying describes something as being "as southern as fried chicken." Certainly no one knows as much about cooking chicken – or any other poultry – as southern homemakers. It just follows naturally that their poultry casseroles would be out of this world. And, as you'll see when you read the recipes on the following pages, they are!

Country Captain Chicken is typically southern in its rich flavor and hearty goodness. This delicious combination of chicken, garlic, curry, tomatoes, rice, and almonds is just right for family dining or for that extra-special dinner party. In fact, it's a meal in itself!

Want to experiment with something different? Then you'll enjoy Gai Lo Mein, a casserole which mixes Chinese vegetables and exotic oriental seasonings with stewed chicken for a delicious – and economical – dish you'll enjoy with rice or crisp Chinese noodles.

There is even an answer to the perennial question of what to do with leftover turkey. You'll be delighted with Hot Turkey Salad Souffle. This light-as-a-cloud casserole is so mouth-watering delicious, no one will ever suspect you created it from leftovers!

These recipes are just samples of the wonderfully varied casseroles in the pages that follow – awaiting your cooking enjoyment – and your family's dining pleasure!

CHICKEN SOUFFLE

1 6-lb. hen	6 eggs, beaten
1 tbsp. monosodium glutamate	Salt and pepper to taste
1 pkg. stuffing mix	6 slices toasted bread,
1 1/2 c. butter	crumbled
1 c. flour	1 c. slivered toasted almonds
1 qt. milk	

Place the hen in a kettle and cover with water. Bring to a boil and reduce heat. Simmer until tender, then drain, reserving 6 cups broth. Cool the hen, remove chicken from bones and cut in bite-sized pieces. Add monosodium glutamate. Mix the stuffing mix with 2 cups reserved broth and place in 2 greased 2-quart casseroles. Melt 1 cup butter in a saucepan. Add the flour and mix well. Add milk and remaining broth slowly and cook over low heat until thickened, stirring constantly. Cool slightly and stir into eggs. Add salt and pepper and pour 1/4 of the sauce into each casserole. Add chicken and cover with remaining sauce. Mix bread crumbs with remaining melted butter and almonds and spread over casseroles. Bake at 350 degrees until bubbly. 20 servings.

Dorothy Hixson, Selma, Alabama

CORN BREAD AND CHICKEN

1 hen	1 can mushroom soup
Salt and pepper to taste	2 tbsp. flour

Cook the hen in boiling, salted water until tender. Drain and reserve 2 cups broth. Cool hen and remove chicken from bones. Cut in bite-sized pieces and place in a saucepan. Sprinkle with pepper. Add soup and reserved broth and heat to boiling point. Mix the flour with small amount of water and stir into chicken mixture. Cook until thickened, then pour into buttered baking dish.

Topping

1 c. cornmeal	1 egg, lightly beaten
1 c. flour	1/2 c. milk
3 tsp. baking powder	2 tbsp. melted butter
3/4 tsp. salt	

Sift the dry ingredients together into a bowl and add egg, milk and butter. Mix well and pour over chicken mixture. Bake at 350 degrees for 1 hour. 6 servings.

Pearl Polosky, Tucson, Arizona

FRANKLY FANCY BUFFET CHICKEN

1 sm. fat hen	Pepper to taste
Salt to taste	Sage to taste
1 med. onion	3 tbsp. flour
1 loaf day-old bread,	4 eggs, beaten
crumbled	Milk
4 hard-cooked eggs, chopped	

Cook the hen in boiling, salted water until tender. Drain and reserve the broth. Chill the reserved broth and cool the hen. Remove chicken from bones and cut in small pieces. Remove fat from the broth and reserve. Cook the onion in 1/4 cup reserved fat in a saucepan until tender. Add the bread, chopped eggs, salt, pepper and sage and mix well. Add enough broth to moisten and spread in a 9 x 15-inch baking pan. Cover with chicken. Melt 3 tablespoons chicken fat in a saucepan and stir in the flour. Mix the beaten eggs with remaining broth and enough milk to make 1 quart liquid and add to flour mixture, stirring constantly. Cook for 3 minutes, stirring frequently, and pour over chicken. Bake at 350 degrees until heated through.

Alberta R. Fox, Maplewood, Louisiana

HUNTINGTON CHICKEN

1 sm. hen	1 pkg. noodles
1 can whole mushrooms	1 sm. can pimento, chopped
1 c. chopped celery	1 can mushroom soup
1 c. chopped onions	1/2 lb. grated cheese
1 c. chopped bell pepper	

Cook the hen in boiling, salted water until tender. Drain and reserve broth. Cool the hen and remove chicken from bones. Drain the mushrooms and reserve liquid. Mix the reserved mushroom liquid and reserved broth in a saucepan. Add the celery, onions and bell pepper and cook until tender. Add the chicken and mushrooms. Cook the noodles according to package directions and add to chicken mixture. Mix in remaining ingredients and place in a large casserole. Bake in 350-degree oven until bubbly.

Bessie Foreman, Forest, Mississippi

CHICKEN RAVIOLI

1 5 to 7-lb. hen, cooked	2 c. chicken broth
2 lge. onions, chopped	1 med. can pimento, cut in
Chopped green pepper to taste	strips
1 c. chopped celery	2 pkg. noodles
2 3-oz. cans sliced	Salt and pepper to taste
mushrooms	1 c. grated mild Cheddar
2 tbsp. butter or margarine	cheese
2 cans cream of mushroom	1 c. toasted croutons
soup	

Remove chicken from bones. Saute the onions, green pepper, celery and mushrooms in butter in a heavy skillet for 5 minutes or until tender. Combine the soup, broth and pimento. Cook the noodles according to package directions and place in a large mixing bowl. Add the chicken, soup mixture and sauteed ingredients and mix well. Add the salt and pepper. Pour into a greased large baking dish and top with cheese and croutons. Bake at 350 degrees for 25 minutes. 10 servings.

Mrs. Louise Spears, Norphlet, Arkansas

CHICKEN-NUT CASSEROLE

1 c. chopped celery
1 c. chopped onion
2 c. chopped cooked chicken
1 can cream of mushroom soup
1 c. water

1 can Chinese noodles
1/4 lb. coarsely chopped
 cashew nuts
1 c. crushed potato chips

Combine all ingredients except potato chips and place in a greased baking dish. Place potato chip crumbs on top. Bake at 325 degrees for 1 hour. 6 servings.

Mrs. Vaughn Fox, Dandridge, Tennessee

ORIENTAL CHICKEN CASSEROLE

1 c. sliced celery
1/2 c. 1/2-in. green onion
 slices
1/3 c. butter
1/4 c. flour
1 tsp. salt
Dash of garlic salt
2 c. milk

2 tsp. soy sauce
1/2 c. shredded American
 process cheese
2 c. cubed cooked chicken
1 8-oz. can water chestnuts
1 6-oz. can chow mein
 noodles

Saute the celery and onion in butter in a saucepan until onion is soft. Blend in the flour, salt and garlic salt. Add the milk and soy sauce and cook, stirring constantly, until thickened. Remove from heat. Add the cheese and stir until melted. Stir in the chicken. Drain the water chestnuts and slice. Stir into chicken mixture. Place layers of noodles and chicken mixture in a 1 1/2-quart casserole, beginning and ending with noodles. Bake at 375 degrees for 25 to 30 minutes or until hot and bubbly. 6 servings.

Oriental Chicken Casserole (above)

CHOPSTICK CHICKEN

1 pkg. frozen chicken breasts	1/4 c. chopped onion
1 can cream of mushroom soup	1 3-oz. can chow mein
1/4 can water	noodles
1 c. chopped celery	1 sm. can mandarin orange
1/4 c. salted cashews, chopped	slices, drained

Cook the chicken breasts in boiling, salted water for 30 minutes. Remove skin and bones and cut chicken in bite-sized pieces. Add the soup, water, celery, cashews, onion and half the noodles and place in a 2-quart casserole. Sprinkle remaining noodles in ring around edge of casserole and cover center with mandarin orange slices. Bake at 350 degrees for 30 minutes or until heated through. 4-6 servings.

Mrs. Robert C. Shaver, Fort Gordon, Georgia

AVOCADO-CHICKEN-SPAGHETTI CASSEROLE

8 oz. broken thin spaghetti	1 c. cubed avocado
1 can cream of celery soup	Salt and pepper to taste
1/4 c. chopped pimento	1/2 c. grated cheese
1 1/2 c. diced cooked chicken	1/3 c. buttered bread crumbs
2 tbsp. butter or margarine	

Cook the spaghetti according to package directions until just tender and drain. Add the soup, pimento, chicken and butter and place in buttered 1 1/2-quart casserole. Fold in avocado, salt and pepper and sprinkle with cheese and bread crumbs. Broil for 3 to 4 minutes or until brown. 4-6 servings.

Mrs. Lionel S. Carpenter, Ft. Myers, Florida

CHICKEN MONTEGO

3 to 4 tbsp. flour	1 can cream of celery soup
1 tsp. salt	1 tsp. ground marjoram
1/8 tsp. pepper	2 c. sour cream
3 chicken breasts, split	1 4-oz. package spaghetti
1/4 c. shortening	twists
1 4-oz. can button	1 16-oz. can sm. peas
mushrooms	

Mix the flour, salt and pepper and dredge chicken breasts with flour mixture. Cook in shortening in a skillet over moderate heat until lightly browned and remove from skillet. Drain the mushrooms and add to skillet. Cook until lightly browned. Add soup and marjoram and mix well. Add sour cream gradually and stir until blended. Cook the spaghetti according to package directions and place in a 3-quart shallow baking dish. Drain the peas and add to spaghetti. Stir in half the soup mixture. Arrange chicken over spaghetti mixture and pour remaining soup mixture over chicken. Cover. Bake at 350 degrees for 45 minutes. Remove cover and bake for 15 minutes longer or until chicken is tender. Garnish with paprika. 6 servings.

Margery G. Middlebrooks, Jonesboro, Georgia

GOURMET RIPE OLIVE POULET

6 boned whole chicken breasts	2 tsp. cornstarch
2 tbsp. chopped chives	2 tbsp. lemon juice
1 1/2 c. canned pitted ripe	2 4 3/4-oz. jars strained
olives	apricots
Garlic salt to taste	3 tbsp. brandy
2 tbsp. melted butter	

Preheat oven to 400 degrees. Place the chicken breasts, skin side down, on a flat surface and sprinkle each with 1 teaspoon chives. Arrange 4 olives in center of each chicken breast and fold chicken around olives. Cut remaining olives in half and reserve. Fasten the chicken breasts with small skewers and sprinkle with garlic salt. Place in butter in a baking dish. Bake for 30 minutes. Mix the cornstarch and lemon juice with apricots in a saucepan and bring to boiling point, stirring frequently. Stir in brandy. Remove the chicken from oven and turn. Spoon apricot sauce over chicken and bake for 20 minutes. Add reserved olives and bake for 5 minutes longer. 6 servings.

Photograph for this recipe on page 80.

COUNTRY CAPTAIN CHICKEN

2 fryers, disjointed	1 1/2 tsp. salt
Seasoned flour	1/2 tsp. pepper
1/2 c. shortening	1/2 tsp. thyme
2 onions, finely chopped	2 1-lb. 3-oz. cans tomatoes
2 green peppers, chopped	1 tbsp. chopped parsley
1 clove of garlic,	6 c. hot cooked rice
minced (opt.)	1/4 c. currants
3 to 4 tsp. curry powder	1/4 lb. toasted almonds

Dredge the chicken with seasoned flour and fry in shortening in a skillet until browned. Remove chicken and keep warm. Cook the onions, green peppers and garlic in remaining shortening in skillet until tender. Stir in the curry powder, salt, pepper and thyme and mix well. Add the tomatoes and parsley and heat through. Place chicken in a large casserole and pour tomato mixture over chicken. Cover. Bake at 350 degrees for 45 minutes or until chicken is tender. Place the chicken on a serving platter and mound rice around chicken. Sprinkle currants in tomato sauce and pour over rice. Sprinkle almonds over chicken.

Mrs. J. E. Oliver, Turbeville, Virginia

CUBAN CHICKEN CASSEROLE

1 1 1/2-lb. chicken,	1 clove of garlic, minced
disjointed	8 stuffed olives, sliced
1/3 c. oil	1 can tomatoes
1 c. rice	1 can English peas
1 onion, chopped	1 tsp. salt
1 green pepper, diced	1/2 tsp. pepper

Brown the chicken in oil in a skillet and remove from skillet. Cool and remove chicken from bones. Place in a casserole and cover with rice. Saute the onion, green pepper and garlic in remaining oil in the skillet. Add remaining ingredients and simmer for 5 minutes. Pour over chicken mixture and cover. Bake at 350 degrees for 1 hour and 15 minutes. 6 servings.

Mrs. Milton S. Woods, Owings, South Carolina

CHICKEN CHARTREUSE

2 c. rice	Salt and pepper to taste
Chicken broth	1 diced cooked hen
2 cans cream of mushroom soup	2 c. dry bread crumbs
1 tbsp. minced onion	Chicken fat

Cook the rice according to package directions, substituting chicken broth for water. Add the soup, onion, salt, pepper and hen and pour into a buttered baking dish. Saute the bread crumbs in small amount of chicken fat until brown and spread over chicken mixture. Bake at 350 degrees for about 30 minutes. 20 servings.

Mrs. W. H. Morris, Alamogordo, New Mexico

ROLLED CITRUS CHICKEN

6 boned whole chicken breasts	1 tbsp. tarragon
6 slices cooked ham	2 tsp. grated orange rind
2/3 c. fine bread crumbs	1/2 tsp. salt
2 c. orange juice	Cooked rice
1 tbsp. melted butter	

Remove skin from chicken breasts and place chicken breasts on a flat surface. Place 1 slice ham on each chicken breast. Roll up and secure with wooden picks. Sprinkle with bread crumbs and place in a shallow baking dish. Bake at 400 degrees for about 15 minutes, turning once. Combine the orange juice, butter, tarragon, grated rind and salt and pour over chicken. Reduce temperature to 350 degrees and bake for about 30 minutes longer, turning occasionally. Serve with rice. 6 servings.

Rolled Citrus Chicken (above)

CHICKEN-TACO CASSEROLE

1 3-lb. chicken, disjointed
2 cans enchilada sauce
1 can mushroom soup
1 lge. onion, chopped
1/2 tsp. garlic salt

Dash of pepper
1 sm. package corn chips,
   crushed
1 c. grated cheese

Cook the chicken in boiling, salted water until tender. Drain and reserve 1 cup broth. Cut chicken in bite-sized pieces. Combine the chicken, enchilada sauce, soup, onion, garlic salt and pepper. Place half the corn chips in a greased baking dish. Add chicken mixture and sprinkle with cheese. Cover with remaining corn chips and pour reserved broth over top. Bake at 350 degrees for about 30 minutes. 6-8 servings.

Mrs. Ersel Tice, Logan, Oklahoma

CHICKEN AND CORN CASSEROLE

1 1/2 c. cracker crumbs
2 c. canned whole kernel corn
2 c. diced cooked chicken
1/2 tsp. salt
1/8 tsp. pepper

2 eggs, slightly beaten
1 c. milk
1/4 c. grated cheese
2 tbsp. melted butter

Line bottom and sides of heavily greased casserole with 1 cup cracker crumbs. Add alternate layers of corn and chicken, then add salt and pepper. Mix the eggs and milk and pour over the chicken mixture. Cover with remaining cracker crumbs, cheese and butter. Bake at 350 degrees until brown. 4-6 servings.

Mrs. Ira Waits, Bienville, Louisiana

CHICKEN-GREEN BEAN CASSEROLE

1 can cream of mushroom soup
1/2 c. milk
1 tsp. salt
1 14 1/2-oz. can chop suey
   vegetables, drained
3 c. chopped cooked chicken
1/3 c. chopped onion

2 9-oz. packages frozen
   green beans
1 1/2 c. grated Cheddar
   cheese
1 3 1/2-oz. can French-fried
   onions

Blend the soup with milk and salt in a bowl. Mix in remaining ingredients except the French-fried onions and place in a 12 x 7 1/2 x 2-inch baking dish. Bake at 350 degrees for 45 minutes. Top with French-fried onions and bake for 10 minutes longer. 4-6 servings.

Jo Ann Carter, Folkston, Georgia

HERBED CHICKEN EN CASSEROLE

3 chicken breasts, split	1 5-oz. can water chestnuts
Salt and pepper to taste	1 3-oz. can broiled sliced
1/4 c. butter or margarine	mushrooms, drained
1 can cream of chicken soup	2 tbsp. chopped green peppers
3/4 c. sherry	1/4 tsp. crushed thyme

Season the chicken with salt and pepper and brown in butter in a skillet over low heat. Arrange chicken, skin side up, in 11 1/2 x 7 1/2 x 1 1/2-inch baking dish. Add the soup to drippings in skillet and add sherry slowly, stirring until smooth. Drain and slice the water chestnuts and add to the soup mixture. Add remaining ingredients and heat to boiling point. Pour over chicken and cover with foil. Bake at 350 degrees for 25 minutes. Uncover and bake for 25 to 35 minutes longer or until chicken is tender. 6 servings.

L. F. Dickson, Dallas, Texas

CHICKEN SALAD SURPRISE

2 c. diced cooked chicken	2 tbsp. lemon juice
2 c. diced celery	1/2 c. mayonnaise
1/2 c. minced green pepper	1 can cream of chicken soup
2 tbsp. minced pimento	1 c. crushed potato chips
1 tbsp. minced onion	1 c. grated cheese
1 tbsp. Worcestershire sauce	Slivered almonds to taste

Combine all ingredients except potato chips, cheese and almonds and place in a casserole. Top with potato chips and cheese and sprinkle with almonds. Bake at 350 degrees for 25 minutes. 6-8 servings.

Mrs. Hoyt Clark, Angelus, South Carolina

CHICKEN CASSEROLE DELIGHT

2 tbsp. chopped onion	3/4 c. chicken broth
1/2 c. chopped celery	1/2 c. evaporated milk
1/4 c. chopped green pepper	1 c. water
2 tbsp. melted butter or	2 c. diced cooked chicken
margarine	1 1/2 tsp. soy sauce
1/3 c. sifted flour	1 c. chicken-flavored cracker
1/2 tsp. garlic salt	crumbs
1/4 tsp. pepper	1 c. grated sharp cheese

Saute the onion, celery and green pepper in butter in a saucepan until tender. Blend in the flour, garlic salt and pepper. Stir in chicken broth, milk and water and cook over medium heat, stirring, until thick. Fold in the chicken and soy sauce and pour into a lightly greased 1 1/2-quart baking dish. Add cracker crumbs and sprinkle with cheese. Bake at 350 degrees for 20 to 25 minutes. 8 servings.

Mrs. Joe N. Fox, Allensville, Kentucky

CHILI-CHICKEN CASSEROLE

1 hen
1 c. diced celery
1/2 c. diced onion
1 pkg. chicken soup mix

1 pkg. tostados
1 med. can green chilies,
   chopped

Cook the hen in boiling, salted water until tender. Drain and reserve broth. Cool the hen and remove chicken from bones. Add the celery, onion and soup mix to chicken broth and simmer until onion and celery are tender. Place alternate layers of tostados, chicken, chilies and broth mixture in a greased casserole. Bake at 375 degrees for 30 minutes. 4-6 servings.

Mrs. Kathryn Williams, Ruidoso, New Mexico

GREEN CHILI ENCHILADA

1 cooked boned 3-lb. chicken
1 can cream of mushroom soup
1 can cream of celery soup
1 sm. can evaporated milk
1 c. chicken broth

1 4-oz. can green chilies,
   chopped
12 tortillas, broken
Grated longhorn cheese

Place the chicken in a large casserole. Add remaining ingredients except cheese and stir well. Cover with cheese. Bake at 400 degrees for 35 to 40 minutes. 6 servings.

Mrs. Elvis Melvin, Loving, New Mexico

CHICKEN SOPA

1 frying chicken
Salt to taste
1 12-oz. package tortillas
1 4-oz. can green chili
   peppers

1 can cream of chicken soup
5 oz. Old English cheese
5 oz. Cheddar cheese
6 to 8 green onions, chopped

Cook the chicken in boiling, salted water until tender. Drain and reserve broth. Cool the chicken, remove from bones and cut in large pieces. Fry tortillas in small amount of fat until soft. Chop the chili peppers. Mix the chicken soup, reserved broth, cheeses, chili peppers and onions in a saucepan and heat until cheeses melt. Layer the tortillas, chicken and sauce in a 2-quart casserole until all ingredients are used. Bake at 325 degrees for 20 minutes. 12 servings.

Mrs. J. L. Knoz, Eden, Texas

KING RANCH TRAIL DRIVE DISH

1 hen
1 sm. onion
1 stalk celery

1 can cream of mushroom soup
1 can cream of chicken soup
1/2 can tomatoes

| 1 chopped onion | 1/4 pkg. chili mix |
| 1 doz. tortillas | 1 c. grated Cheddar cheese |

Place the hen in a kettle and add whole onion and celery. Cover with water and bring to a boil. Reduce heat and simmer until tender. Drain and reserve 2 cups broth. Remove chicken from bones and cut in chunks. Combine the soups, tomatoes and chopped onion. Break the tortillas into pieces and place in a casserole. Add the chicken, then add soup mixture. Sprinkle with chili mix and add reserved broth. Sprinkle with cheese. Bake at 350 degrees for 45 minutes to 1 hour.

Mrs. J. J. Stephen, Robston, Texas

CHICKEN CASSEROLE WITH ASPARAGUS

1 4-oz. can sliced mushrooms	1 tall can evaporated milk
1/4 c. butter	1 c. diced cooked chicken
1/4 c. chopped onion	1 3-oz. can chow mein
1/4 c. flour	noodles
1 tsp. salt	1 10-oz. package frozen cut
Dash of pepper	asparagus
1/2 tsp. curry powder	1 c. grated cheese

Preheat oven to 350 degrees. Drain the mushrooms and reserve liquid. Melt the butter in a large frypan. Add the mushrooms and onion and cook over medium heat until onion is transparent. Remove from heat. Add the flour, salt, pepper and curry powder and stir until blended. Add enough water to reserved mushroom liquid to make 1/2 cup liquid and add to mushroom mixture slowly, stirring constantly. Blend in milk and cook over medium heat, stirring, until thickened. Add chicken and noodles. Cook the asparagus according to package directions and drain. Add to chicken mixture and mix. Turn into a greased 1 1/2-quart casserole and top with cheese. Bake for 20 to 30 minutes or until heated through and cheese is melted. 5-6 servings.

Chicken Casserole with Asparagus (above)

CHICKEN BREASTS WITH ARTICHOKES

4 chicken breasts, halved	1 can chicken broth
1 lge. onion, thinly sliced	1 can artichokes, drained
1/2 c. chopped bell pepper	Salt and pepper to taste
1/2 c. salad oil	1 4-oz. can button
Juice of 1 lemon	mushrooms
1 c. rice	12 stuffed olives, sliced

Saute chicken breasts, onion and bell pepper in oil in a skillet until brown and drizzle lemon juice over chicken breasts. Cook the rice in chicken broth in a saucepan until tender and add remaining ingredients, being careful to keep artichokes whole. Place in a greased 8-inch square casserole and place chicken mixture on top. Cover. Bake at 325 degrees for 1 hour. Garnish with toasted almonds, if desired. 6-8 servings.

Mrs. Bennie Ward, Lambert, Mississippi

CHICKEN SPECIAL CASSEROLE

6 chicken breasts	3/4 c. slivered almonds
2 stalks celery, chopped	3 cans mushroom soup
3 cans asparagus pieces	2 cans French-fried onion
1 sm. can pimentos, chopped	rings

Cook the chicken breasts with celery in boiling, salted water in a saucepan until tender. Drain chicken. Remove chicken from bones and cut in bite-sized pieces. Place alternate layers of chicken, asparagus, pimentos, almonds and soup in a casserole and cover with foil. Bake at 350 degrees for 25 minutes. Uncover and top with onion rings. Bake for 5 minutes longer. 6-8 servings.

Mrs. Hugh Colville, Jr., Bessemer, Alabama

CHICKEN DIVAN PARISIAN

1 can cream of celery soup	1 tsp. Worcestershire sauce
1/4 c. milk	2 pkg. frozen broccoli
1/4 tsp. nutmeg	2 c. sliced cooked chicken
1 c. heavy cream	1 c. grated Parmesan cheese
1/2 c. mayonnaise	

Mix the soup, milk and nutmeg in a saucepan and heat through. Combine the heavy cream, mayonnaise and Worcestershire sauce in a bowl and stir in the soup mixture. Cook the broccoli according to package directions and drain. Place in a shallow casserole in single layer. Spoon half the soup mixture over broccoli and cover with chicken. Add remaining soup mixture and sprinkle with cheese. Bake at 350 degrees for 20 minutes or until bubbly. 6-8 servings.

Mrs. W. Murray Smith, Clay, West Virginia

CHICKEN-AVOCADO CASSEROLE

1 6-lb. chicken, quartered	1/2 c. grated Cheddar cheese
1 med. onion, chopped	1/8 tsp. rosemary
1/2 c. diced celery	1/8 tsp. basil
4 tsp. salt	1/8 tsp. hot sauce
1 tbsp. pepper	1/2 lb. sliced broiled
1 qt. water	mushrooms
2 tbsp. butter	2 ripe avocados, diced
3 tbsp. flour	1/2 c. toasted slivered
1 c. light cream	almonds

Place the chicken, onion, celery, 1 tablespoon salt, pepper and water in a large kettle and bring to a boil. Reduce heat and simmer until the chicken is tender. Remove chicken from broth and cool. Remove all chicken except wings and neck from bones. Place wings and neck back into broth and simmer for 30 minutes. Drain and reserve stock. Melt the butter in a saucepan and blend in the flour. Add 1 cup reserved stock and cream and cook, stirring, until thick. Add the cheese, remaining salt, rosemary, basil and hot sauce. Place the chicken in a 3-quart casserole and cover with mushrooms. Pour cheese sauce over mushrooms and cover. Bake at 350 degrees for 25 minutes. Uncover and add avocados. Bake for 15 minutes longer and sprinkle with almonds just before serving. 8 servings.

Mrs. Estell Shalla, Bay City, Texas

CHICKEN AND CORN PUDDING

2 c. diced cooked chicken	1/8 tsp. pepper
3 eggs, well beaten	1/4 c. minced onion
3 c. milk	1/4 c. minced green pepper
2 tbsp. flour	1 3/4 c. canned whole kernel
1 1/2 tsp. salt	corn

Place the chicken in a greased casserole. Beat the eggs, milk and flour together in a bowl and add remaining ingredients. Pour over chicken. Bake at 325 degrees for 1 hour or longer. 6-8 servings.

Mrs. Peggy Fowler Revels, Woodruff, South Carolina

CHICKEN OLIVETTE

2 c. corn flakes	1/4 c. chopped ripe olives
2 tbsp. melted butter or	2 tbsp. chopped pimento
margarine	3/4 c. salad dressing
2 tbsp. chopped green onions	1/2 tsp. salt
3/4 c. chopped celery	2 c. diced cooked chicken

Crush the corn flakes and mix with butter. Combine the onions, celery, olives, pimento, salad dressing and salt in a large bowl. Add the chicken and stir until mixed. Spread in a 1 1/2-quart casserole and sprinkle with corn flake mixture. Bake at 450 degrees for about 10 minutes.

Mrs. Lucille Alvey, Lindale, Texas

Deep-Dish Plantation Pie (below)

DEEP-DISH PLANTATION PIE

1 3-lb. chicken	1 c. sliced cooked carrots
1 c. chopped onion	1 c. cooked peas
1/4 c. butter or margarine	Oregano to taste
2 c. canned applesauce	Pepper to taste
1 tsp. curry powder	5 tbsp. flour
Salt	1 recipe pie pastry

Cook the chicken in boiling, salted water until tender. Drain and reserve 2 cups stock. Remove chicken from bones and cut in large pieces. Saute the onion in butter in a saucepan until light brown and add the applesauce, curry powder and 1/4 teaspoon salt. Cook, stirring occasionally, until slightly thickened, then pour into a 7 1/2 x 12 x 2-inch baking dish. Combine the carrots and peas and spoon over the applesauce mixture. Place the chicken over the carrot mixture and sprinkle with oregano, salt to taste and pepper. Mix the flour with 1/4 cup cold water until smooth and stir into chicken stock in a saucepan. Cook, stirring constantly, until thickened and pour 1/2 cup over chicken. Cover baking dish with pastry and cut slits in pastry to allow steam to escape. Flute edge of pastry. Bake at 400 degrees for 45 minutes or until pastry is browned. Serve hot with remaining gravy. 6 servings.

COUNTRY CHICKEN DINNER

1 lge. hen	2 c. diced celery
1 can tomato soup	1 c. diced carrots
1 can cream of mushroom soup	1 c. rice
1 No. 2 can sm. English peas	2 tsp. salt
1 No. 2 can tomatoes	1/2 tsp. pepper
2 onions, diced	1 tsp. paprika

Cook the hen in boiling water in a large kettle until tender. Drain and reserve broth. Cool hen. Remove chicken from bones and cut in large pieces. Place a layer of chicken in a 2 1/2-quart casserole. Combine the soups and vegetables and place a layer of vegetable mixture over chicken. Continue layers until all chicken and vegetable mixture are used. Soak the rice in hot water for 10 minutes, then drain. Sprinkle on chicken mixture. Add seasonings and cover. Bake at 350 degrees until rice is done, adding reserved broth as needed. 12-16 servings.

Mrs. Luther Rice, Wedowee, Alabama

FIX-AHEAD CHICKEN

2 lb. chicken parts	Dash of pepper
2 tbsp. shortening	4 med. carrots
1 can cream of chicken soup	6 sm. onions
1/2 soup can milk	1 10-oz. package frozen
1/4 tsp. poultry seasoning	lima beans
1/4 tsp. salt	

Brown the chicken in shortening in a skillet and place in a 2-quart casserole. Discard the drippings. Mix the soup, milk and seasonings in the skillet and heat through. Cut the carrots lengthwise in quarters and add to the soup mixture. Add the onions and cover. Cook over low heat for 10 minutes, stirring frequently. Add the lima beans and cook until separated, stirring frequently. Pour over the chicken. Cover and refrigerate until chilled. Bake in a 375-degree oven for 1 hour. Uncover and bake for 15 minutes longer or until chicken is tender. Decrease baking time of covered casserole 15 minutes if not refrigerated before baking. 4 servings.

Fix-Ahead Chicken (above)

Baked Chicken with Peaches (below)

BAKED CHICKEN WITH PEACHES

1 fryer, quartered	**1 tbsp. butter or margarine**
1 tbsp. flour	**1 1-lb. can peach halves**
1 tsp. monosodium glutamate	**1/2 tsp. cinnamon**
1/2 tsp. salt	**1/2 tsp. nutmeg**

Place the chicken in a shallow baking dish. Combine the flour, monosodium glutamate and salt and sprinkle over the chicken. Dot with butter. Bake at 375 degrees for 30 minutes. Drain the peaches and reserve 1/2 cup syrup. Place the peach halves around chicken. Spoon reserved syrup over chicken and peaches and sprinkle with cinnamon and nutmeg. Bake for 20 minutes longer. 6 servings.

TROPICAL CHICKEN

3 tbsp. butter	**1 1/2 c. diced cooked chicken**
4 tbsp. flour	**1/2 c. diced pineapple**
1 c. chicken broth	**1/2 c. chopped pecans**
1 c. milk	**Grated Parmesan cheese**
1/2 tsp. salt	**Parlsey sprigs**
1/2 tsp. paprika	

Melt the butter in top of a double boiler. Add flour and stir over low heat until blended. Add broth and milk all at once and cook, stirring constantly, until thickened. Place over hot water and add seasonings and chicken. Heat through. Blend in pineapple and pour into a 1-quart casserole. Top with pecans. Cover with cheese. Bake at 350 degrees until lightly browned, then garnish with parsley. 6 servings.

Noretta Hampton, Virgie, Kentucky

TURKEY AND NOODLE CASSEROLE

2 c. medium noodles	1/2 c. milk
1 pkg. frozen broccoli	1 1/2 c. grated Cheddar cheese
2 c. diced cooked turkey	1/2 tsp. prepared mustard
1 can celery soup	1/2 c. chopped pimentos

Cook the noodles and broccoli according to package directions and drain. Dice the broccoli stems and leave flowerets whole. Place the noodles in a large casserole and add broccoli stems. Add the turkey. Mix the soup, milk, cheese and mustard in a saucepan and heat through. Pour over the turkey and add pimentos. Arrange broccoli flowerets on top. Bake at 350 degrees for 45 minutes.

Mrs. E. E. Washburn, Harrisville, West Virginia

HOT TURKEY SALAD SOUFFLE

6 thin slices bread	3/4 tsp. salt
2 c. diced cooked turkey	Dash of pepper
1/2 c. chopped onion	2 eggs, beaten
1/2 c. chopped green pepper	1 1/2 c. milk
1/2 c. finely chopped celery	1 c. cream of mushroom soup
1/2 c. mayonnaise	1/2 c. shredded cheese

Cut 2 slices bread in cubes and place in 8 x 8 x 2-inch baking dish. Combine the turkey, vegetables, mayonnaise and seasonings and place over bread cubes. Trim crusts from remaining bread and arrange on turkey mixture. Mix the eggs and milk and pour over bread. Cover with foil and chill for at least 1 hour or overnight. Spoon mushroom soup over top. Bake at 325 degrees for 1 hour or until set. Sprinkle with cheese and bake for 15 minutes longer or until brown. 6 servings.

TURKEY CASSEROLE

3 tbsp. chopped onion	1 can cream of chicken soup
1/3 c. chopped green pepper	1 c. chopped cooked turkey
3 tbsp. melted fat	1 tbsp. lemon juice
1 tsp. salt	1 pkg. refrigerator biscuits
6 tbsp. flour	1/3 c. grated cheese
1 1/2 c. milk	

Preheat oven to 450 degrees. Brown the onion and green pepper in fat in a saucepan. Add the salt and flour and blend. Add the milk and soup and cook until thick, stirring occasionally. Add the turkey and lemon juice and pour into a greased casserole. Roll biscuits to form a rectangle 1/4 inch thick and sprinkle with grated cheese. Roll as for jelly roll and cut in 1/2-inch thick slices. Place on turkey mixture. Bake for 15 minutes. Reduce temperature to 425 degrees and bake until swirls are browned. One recipe biscuit dough may be substituted for refrigerator biscuits. 6 servings.

Mrs. Mildred Tate, Lobelville, Tennessee

fish & shellfish

The fortunate southern homemaker has ready access to plentiful supplies of seafood — the rich water of the Gulf and the Atlantic and the teeming fresh-water streams and lakes which dot the southern landscape provide an infinite variety of fish and shellfish.

The recipes you will find in the following section match this variety. From the Creole-flavored cooking of the bayou country has come Seafood Louisiana, a sharply flavored combination of seasonings, vegetables, scallops, and oysters.

Planning a party? What could be more delicious — or easier to fix — than Lobster Casserole Supreme. The delicate flavor of lobster combines delightfully with mushrooms and cheese in this delicious casserole.

For those in-a-hurry suppers, try Deviled Salmon Supper Delight — just half an hour from cupboard to table. Another quick and easy favorite is Tuna and Cheese Casserole. This mouth-watering combination of cheese, egg, and tuna fish has the extra bonus of being rich in needed protein . . . and easy on your budget!

Hearty and nutritious fish and shellfish casseroles are certain to become favorites with your family. And the recipes in this section will become as cherished by you as they are by the southern homemakers who proudly share them with you.

101

MUSHROOM SEAFARERS CASSEROLE

3/4 lb. fresh mushrooms	1 7-oz. package frozen
1 12-oz. package frozen	cleaned shrimp
halibut steak, thawed	1/4 tsp. ground thyme
1 10 1/2-oz. can chicken	1/4 tsp. salt
gumbo soup	1/4 tsp. hot sauce
1 1-lb. can tomatoes, drained	4 c. cooked rice

Rinse, pat dry and halve the mushrooms and set aside. Remove bones and skin from the halibut and cut halibut in 2-inch chunks. Place the soup and tomatoes in a medium saucepan and bring to boiling point. Add the mushrooms, halibut, shrimp, thyme, salt and hot sauce and mix. Pour into a casserole. Bake at 350 degrees for 20 to 25 minutes or until halibut and shrimp are done. Surround with a ring of rice and garnish with parsley, if desired. Two 6-ounce cans sliced mushrooms, drained, may be substituted for fresh mushrooms. 6 servings.

Photograph for this recipe on page 100.

BAKED WHITEFISH ON CELERY LEAVES

Celery leaves	1 1/2 c. mayonnaise
4 thick fillets of whitefish	1/2 c. pickle relish
4 tbsp. lemon juice	3 green onions, chopped
1/2 tsp. salt	1 tbsp. chopped parsley
1/4 tsp. white pepper	1/4 c. chopped macadamia nuts
Paprika to taste	

Cover the bottom of a shallow casserole with celery leaves. Sprinkle fillets with lemon juice, then with salt, pepper and paprika. Let stand for 20 minutes and place on celery leaves. Mix remaining ingredients except nuts and spread over fillets. Sprinkle macadamia nuts over top. Bake in 350-degree oven for 25 to 30 minutes. Chopped almonds may be substituted for macadamia nuts.

Mrs. Harvey Plumlee, Reno, Nevada

FISH CASSEROLE

1 green pepper, chopped	1 c. buttered soft bread
3 tbsp. butter	crumbs
2 tbsp. flour	Salt and pepper to taste
1 1/2 c. cream	Sherry to taste
1 c. flaked cooked fish	

Saute the green pepper in butter in a saucepan until tender. Add flour and blend until smooth. Stir in the cream and cook, stirring, until thick and smooth. Add the fish, 1/2 cup crumbs, salt, pepper and sherry and mix well. Pour into a baking dish and cover with remaining crumbs. Bake at 375 degrees until brown. 4 servings.

Mrs. Griffis Meek, Grenada, Mississippi

NEWFOUNDLAND FISH CASSEROLE

2 lb. haddock fillets
1 tbsp. chopped onion
1 tbsp. Worcestershire sauce
2 tbsp. melted butter
2 tbsp. flour

1 1/2 c. milk
1/4 tsp. salt
Pepper to taste
3 c. hot mashed potatoes
1/2 c. grated cheese

Simmer the fillets in boiling, salted water in a saucepan for 10 minutes. Drain and flake. Place in a 2-quart casserole and add the onion, Worcestershire sauce and butter. Add the flour and blend. Add milk gradually and cook until smooth and thick, stirring constantly. Add the salt and pepper and top with potatoes and cheese. Bake at 375 degrees for 25 minutes.

Mrs. A. B. Davidson, Moultrie, Georgia

FILLETS OF FISH

4 fish fillets
1 1/2 tsp. salt
Pepper to taste
Thyme to taste
1 can mussels in water

2 yellow onions, sliced
2 tbsp. butter or margarine
1/2 c. white wine
1/2 c. cream
2 tsp. flour

Cut the fillets in half lengthwise and sprinkle with salt, pepper and thyme. Drain the mussels and reserve liquid. Place a mussel in each fillet half and roll. Place the rolls in a baking dish. Saute the onions in butter in a saucepan until golden brown and place between the rolls in the baking dish. Add reserved mussel liquid and the wine and cover baking dish with foil. Bake at 350 degrees for about 30 minutes. Pour off the liquid carefully into a saucepan and add the cream. Place over low heat. Mix the flour with small amount of water and stir into cream mixture. Cook, stirring, until thickened. Season with additional salt and pepper to taste and pour over fish rolls. Garnish with parsley and serve with rice. 4 servings.

Fillets of Fish (above)

RED SNAPPER A LA CRIOLLA

2 tbsp. olive oil
1 lge. onion, sliced
5 tomatoes, peeled and sliced
Salt and pepper to taste
2 lb. boned red snapper

1 tbsp. vinegar
3 cloves of garlic, chopped
1/4 tsp. oregano
2 green peppers, sliced
4 canned pimentos, chopped

Rub inside of casserole with 1 tablespoon olive oil. Place half the onion and tomatoes in the casserole and sprinkle with salt and pepper. Add the red snapper. Mix remaining olive oil, vinegar, garlic and oregano and spread over snapper. Sprinkle with salt and pepper. Top with green peppers, pimentos and remaining tomatoes and onion and sprinkle with salt and pepper. Bake at 325 degrees for about 45 minutes or until done. 4 servings.

Mrs. Harold R. Bailey, Marietta, Georgia

ASPARAGUS-SALMON RIVIERA

2 pkg. frozen asparagus
   spears
4 tbsp. butter
3 tbsp. flour

2 c. milk
1 tall can salmon
Salt and pepper to taste
1/4 c. Parmesan cheese

Cook the asparagus according to package directions, drain and place in a greased baking dish. Melt the butter in a saucepan and blend in the flour. Stir in milk and cook, stirring, until thick. Drain and flake the salmon and stir into white sauce. Stir in seasonings and pour over asparagus. Top with the Parmesan cheese. Bake at 350 degrees for 15 to 20 minutes and garnish with lemon and parsley. 8-10 servings.

Mrs. S. L. Norrell, Cleburne, Texas

DEVILED SALMON SUPPER DELIGHT

6 hard-cooked eggs
1 tsp. Worcestershire sauce
1/4 tsp. hot sauce
1/2 tsp. dry mustard
1/2 c. sour cream

2 tbsp. minced chives
1 7 3/4-oz. can salmon
1 can spaghetti with
   tomato and cheese sauce

Preheat oven to 375 degrees. Cut the eggs in half and remove yolks. Mash the egg yolks and add the Worcestershire sauce, hot sauce and mustard. Stir in the sour cream and chives. Drain and flake the salmon and fold into egg yolk mixture. Stuff egg whites with salmon mixture, piling high in center. Place spaghetti in a shallow casserole and top with stuffed eggs and any remaining salmon mixture. Bake for 15 minutes. Green onion tops may be substituted for chives. 4 servings.

Jeanne Owens Glassock, Celeste, Texas

SALMON CASSEROLE WITH BUTTERMILK BISCUITS

1 tbsp. minced onion	2 tbsp. chopped parsley
1/4 c. minced celery	Salt to taste
3 tbsp. butter	1/8 tsp. cayenne pepper
1/4 c. flour	1/4 tsp. thyme
1 1-lb. can salmon	1 4-oz. can mushroom
Milk	pieces
1/4 c. cream	1 1-lb. can tiny peas

Saute the onion and celery in butter in a saucepan for 3 minutes or until onion is transparent. Stir in the flour and cook for 2 minutes, stirring constantly. Drain the salmon and reserve liquid. Add enough milk to reserved liquid to make 1 1/2 cups liquid. Add to onion mixture slowly and cook until thickened, stirring constantly. Stir in the cream, parsley, seasonings and salmon. Drain the mushrooms and stir into salmon mixture. Drain the peas and reserve 1/4 cup. Place remaining peas in a greased 1 1/2-quart casserole and pour salmon mixture over peas.

Buttermilk Biscuits

2 c. flour	1 tsp. salt
1 tsp. soda	1/3 c. shortening
1 tsp. baking powder	2/3 c. buttermilk

Combine the flour, soda, baking powder and salt in a bowl and cut in shortening with pastry blender until consistency of fine meal. Add the buttermilk and mix well. Turn out on a lightly floured board and knead about 12 times. Roll out 1/2 inch thick and cut with small biscuit cutter. Place around edge of casserole. Bake at 425 degrees for 20 to 25 minutes or until biscuits are well browned. Place reserved peas in center of casserole.

Salmon Casserole with Buttermilk Biscuits (above)

BAKED SALMON CASSEROLE

1 sm. onion, chopped	1 lge. can evaporated milk
1/2 green pepper, chopped	2 pieces of toasted bread,
Butter	crumbled
1 can pink salmon, flaked	Salt and pepper to taste

Cook the onion and green pepper in small amount of butter in a saucepan for about 10 minutes. Combine the salmon, milk, toast crumbs, onion mixture, salt and pepper and mix well. Place in a greased baking dish. Bake at 400 degrees for 30 minutes.

Mrs. Evelyn Garber, Harrisonburg, Virginia

SALMON CASSEROLE

1 c. chopped celery	1 1/4 c. canned whole
1/4 c. chopped green pepper	kernel corn
1/3 c. chopped onion	2 1/2 c. white sauce
1 c. sliced canned mushrooms	1/4 tsp. curry powder
2 tbsp. butter	Dash of pepper
2 c. flaked salmon	6 unbaked biscuits

Cook the celery, green pepper, onion and mushrooms in butter in a saucepan until tender and add the salmon and corn. Combine the white sauce, curry powder and pepper and add to salmon mixture. Turn into a 2-quart casserole and arrange biscuits over salmon mixture. Bake at 425 degrees for 25 to 30 minutes. 6 servings.

Mrs. Robert A. Slater, Hanover, Virginia

SALMON AND TOMATO CASSEROLE

2 tbsp. chopped onion	Dash of pepper
2 tbsp. chopped green pepper	1/2 tbsp. sugar
Shortening	1 8-oz. can salmon, drained
1 tbsp. flour	1 c. grated American cheese
1 1/4 c. canned tomatoes	1/2 recipe biscuit dough
1/4 tsp. salt	

Saute the onion and green pepper in small amount of shortening in a saucepan until tender and stir in flour. Combine the tomatoes, seasonings and sugar and add to flour mixture. Bring to a boil, stirring constantly, and remove from heat. Place the salmon in a shallow casserole and cover with tomato mixture. Sprinkle with cheese. Roll out dough on a floured surface to fit casserole and place on cheese. Cut slits in center of dough. Bake at 400 degrees for 20 to 25 minutes or until crust is done. 4 servings.

Mrs. Louise Watson, Amite, Louisiana

FISHERMAN'S PIE

1/4 c. chopped onion	1 1-lb. can salmon,
1 4-oz. can sliced	drained
mushrooms	Dash of pepper
3 tbsp. butter	1 10-oz. package frozen peas
2 cans celery soup	3 med. cooked potatoes, mashed
1/4 tsp. salt	

Saute the onion and mushrooms in butter in a saucepan for 5 minutes. Add the celery soup, salmon, salt and pepper. Cook the peas according to package directions and drain. Stir into salmon mixture. Turn into a greased 1-quart casserole and spoon potatoes around edge of casserole. Bake in a 350-degree oven for 25 minutes. 4 servings.

Mrs. Curtis Watson, Toccoa, Georgia

MEXICAN TUNA-CHILI POT

2 7-oz. cans tuna in	1 1-lb. can kidney beans
vegetable oil	2 tsp. chili powder
2 tbsp. finely chopped onion	1 12-oz. package corn
1 1-lb. can tomatoes	bread mix

Drain 2 tablespoons oil from tuna into a large skillet. Add the onion and cook until tender but not brown. Add the tomatoes, kidney beans, tuna and chili powder and bring to a boil. Reduce heat and simmer for about 10 minutes. Prepare corn bread mix according to package directions. Pour tuna mixture into a 2-quart casserole. Drop corn bread mixture by rounded tablespoonfuls onto tuna mixture, placing 6 mounds on top. Spoon remaining corn bread mixture into 6 greased 2 1/2-inch muffin cups. Place casserole and muffin pan in oven. Bake at 425 degrees for 15 to 20 minutes or until corn bread is golden brown. 6 servings.

Mexican Tuna-Chili Pot (above)

DEVILED TUNA CASSEROLE

1/3 c. chopped celery	1 10 1/2-oz. can lima beans
2 tbsp. minced onion	2 tsp. prepared mustard
2 tbsp. chopped green pepper	1/2 tsp. salt
3 tbsp. margarine	Dash of pepper
3 tbsp. flour	1 1/2 tsp. Worcestershire
1 1/2 c. milk	sauce
1 7-oz. can tuna	2 drops of hot sauce
1 tbsp. chopped pimento	1 c. crushed potato chips

Cook the celery, onion and green pepper in margarine in a saucepan until tender and blend in the flour. Add milk gradually and cook over low heat, stirring constantly, until thick. Drain the tuna and break into large pieces. Add to sauce. Add the pimento, lima beans, mustard and seasonings and mix well. Pour into baking dish and sprinkle with potato chips. Bake in 400-degree oven for about 20 minutes or until browned. 4 servings.

Mrs. Joseph Basset, New Orleans, Louisiana

TUNA AND LIMA BEAN CASSEROLE

1 pkg. frozen lima beans	1/2 soup can milk
1 can tuna, drained	1/3 lb. Cheddar cheese, sliced
3 hard-cooked eggs, sliced	1/2 c. toasted bread crumbs
1 can cream of mushroom soup	2 tbsp. butter

Cook the lima beans according to package directions and drain. Layer the tuna, eggs, beans, soup, milk and cheese in a baking dish. Sprinkle with crumbs and dot with butter. Bake at 350 degrees for 30 minutes. 4 servings.

Mrs. John J. Taylor, Ocala, Florida

MACARONI WITH TUNA AND CORN

1 pkg. elbow macaroni	1 c. whole kernel corn
2 tbsp. butter	Salt and pepper to taste
2 tbsp. flour	Paprika to taste
2 c. milk	1 c. grated cheese
1 7-oz. can tuna, drained	

Cook the macaroni according to package directions and drain. Melt the butter in a saucepan and stir in the flour. Add milk gradually and cook over low heat until smooth and thick, stirring constantly. Stir in the tuna, corn, seasonings and 1/2 of the cheese. Place alternate layers of tuna mixture and macaroni in a buttered baking dish and sprinkle with remaining cheese. Bake at 350 degrees until brown.

Mary Lou Campbell, Honea Path, South Carolina

TUNA AND CHEESE CASSEROLE

1 pkg. wide noodles	Salt and pepper to taste
1 can tuna	1 can mushroom soup

3/4 c. grated cheese	**3/4 c. milk**
1 egg, beaten	**1/4 c. cracker crumbs**

Cook the noodles according to package directions and place alternate layers of noodles, tuna, salt, pepper and soup in a 1 1/2-quart casserole. Shape cheese into small balls and press into tuna mixture. Mix the egg and milk and pour over tuna mixture. Cover with crumbs. Bake at 350 degrees for 30 to 40 minutes. 6 servings.

Mrs. Fred Jones, Kilmichael, Mississippi

HOT TUNA SALAD PIE

3 7-oz. cans tuna in vegetable oil	**1 tbsp. lemon juice**
1 c. chopped celery	**1 tsp. Worcestershire sauce**
1 c. finely cubed bread	**1/2 tsp. dry mustard**
1/2 c. chopped pecans	**1/4 tsp. hot sauce**
2 tbsp. minced onion	**1 baked 9-in. pastry shell**
1/2 c. mayonnaise	**1 c. grated Cheddar cheese**

Combine the tuna, celery, bread, pecans and onion in a bowl. Mix the mayonnaise, lemon juice, Worcestershire sauce, mustard and hot sauce and toss lightly with tuna mixture. Turn into the pastry shell. Bake in 350-degree oven for 40 to 45 minutes or until heated through. Sprinkle with cheese and bake for 2 to 3 minutes longer or until cheese is melted. Garnish with sliced stuffed olives, if desired. 6 servings.

Hot Tuna Salad Pie (above)

CREOLE RICE AND TUNA

1 c. rice	2 tbsp. chopped green pepper
2 eggs	1/2 c. chopped celery
1/4 tsp. salt	3 tbsp. soy sauce
2 tbsp. oil	1 7-oz. can tuna
2 tbsp. bacon drippings	Chopped green onions
1 c. chopped onion	

Cook the rice according to package instructions and cool. Beat eggs and salt together. Heat the oil in skillet over moderate heat. Cook eggs in oil as for an omelet. Remove from skillet and cool. Cut in small pieces. Place bacon drippings in the skillet. Add the chopped onion, green pepper and celery and cook until tender-crisp. Add the rice, eggs and soy sauce and stir lightly to mix. Drain and flake the tuna and stir into rice mixture. Place in a casserole. Bake at 425 degrees until heated through. Garnish with green onions. 6-8 servings.

Mrs. Fred Davis, Lamesa, Texas

TUNA SOUFFLE

1 onion, minced	3 eggs, separated
1 tbsp. minced green pepper	1 can light tuna, drained
2 tbsp. butter	and flaked
2 tbsp. flour	Salt and pepper to taste
1 c. milk	

Saute the onion and green pepper in butter in a saucepan until tender and blend in flour. Add milk slowly and remove from heat. Stir in beaten egg yolks. Drain and flake the tuna and stir into onion mixture. Beat the egg whites until stiff and fold into tuna mixture. Add salt and pepper and pour into a casserole. Place casserole in pan of hot water. Bake at 350 degrees for 1 hour.

Mrs. William Guy Reed, Corbin, Kentucky

SCALLOPED TUNA AND CHIPS

1/4 c. shortening	2 tbsp. grated onion
1/4 c. all-purpose flour	1 tbsp. chopped parsley
1 tsp. salt	1 8-oz. package potato
1/8 tsp. pepper	chips
2 c. milk	2 7-oz. cans tuna

Melt the shortening in a saucepan. Add flour, salt and pepper and blend well. Add the milk and cook, stirring constantly until thickened. Remove from heat. Add the onion and parsley and mix well. Crush the potato chips. Place 1/3 of the potato chips in a greased 1 1/2-quart baking dish. Drain and flake the tuna and place half the tuna over potato chips. Add half the sauce. Repeat layers, ending with potato chips. Bake at 350 degrees for 1 hour. 6 servings.

Diane Suggett, Brinkley, Arkansas

SCALLOPED TUNA

2 7-oz. cans tuna	3/4 c. sauteed mushrooms
2 c. crushed cheese crackers	2 hard-cooked eggs, sliced
3 c. medium white sauce	

Preheat oven to 350 degrees. Drain the tuna and break into large pieces. Place alternate layers of cracker crumbs, tuna, white sauce, mushrooms and eggs in a buttered 1 1/2-quart baking dish, beginning and ending with cracker crumbs. Bake for 35 minutes. 6 servings.

Nancy T. Martin, Roxboro, North Carolina

TUNA-CHEESE SOUFFLE

3 tbsp. butter or margarine	1/4 tsp. oregano leaves
1/4 c. flour	1/4 tsp. dry mustard
1 c. milk	1/8 tsp. pepper
1 c. grated Cheddar cheese	4 eggs, separated
1/2 tsp. salt	1 7-oz. can tuna, drained

Melt the butter in a saucepan and blend in the flour. Stir in the milk gradually and cook, stirring constantly, until sauce boils for 1 minute. Add the cheese and seasonings and heat, stirring, until cheese is melted. Beat egg whites until stiff and fold in beaten egg yolks. Fold into cheese mixture. Flake the tuna and fold into cheese mixture. Grease bottom of 1 1/2-quart casserole and pour cheese mixture into casserole. Bake in 350-degree oven for 45 minutes or until knife inserted in center comes out clean. Serve immediately. 6 servings.

HOT TUNA SALAD

2 7-oz. cans tuna, drained	1 tbsp. lemon juice
1 c. chopped celery	1 tbsp. grated onion
1/4 c. sliced ripe pitted olives	1/4 tsp. celery seed
2 tbsp. chopped green pepper	1/2 tsp. salt
2 tbsp. chopped pimento	1/2 c. crushed round buttery crackers
1/2 c. toasted slivered almonds	2 tbsp. grated cheese
2/3 c. mayonnaise	1 tbsp. melted butter or margarine

Combine the tuna, celery, olives, green pepper, pimento and almonds in a bowl and mix well. Mix the mayonnaise, lemon juice, onion, celery seed and salt. Add to tuna mixture and toss lightly. Turn into 8-inch square baking dish. Combine remaining ingredients and sprinkle over top. Bake at 350 degrees for 10 minutes. 5-6 servings.

Mrs. William Strieber, Crofton, Maryland

Scallop Casserole (below)

SCALLOP CASSEROLE

1 lb. sea scallops	1/4 c. diced pimento
6 tbsp. melted margarine	1/4 tsp. salt
3 tbsp. cornstarch	Dash of paprika
2 1/2 c. milk	1/2 c. fine dry bread crumbs
1/2 c. sliced celery	Lemon slices or wedges

Remove any shell particles from the scallops and wash scallops. Blend 4 table-spoons margarine with cornstarch in a saucepan. Stir in milk gradually and mix until smooth. Cook over medium heat until thickened, stirring constantly, then cook for 1 minute. Mix in the scallops, celery, pimento, salt and paprika and pour into a 1 1/2-quart shallow casserole. Mix the bread crumbs and remaining butter and sprinkle on scallop mixture. Bake at 350 degrees for 30 minutes or until heated through. Garnish with lemon slices. 3-4 servings.

EGGPLANT AND CLAMS

1 eggplant	1/4 tsp. onion powder
1 7 1/2-oz. can minced clams	Salt and pepper to taste
	1 1-lb. can cream-style corn
1 c. coarse cracker crumbs	2 eggs, separated
1/4 c. melted butter	1 c. grated Cheddar cheese

Peel the eggplant and cut into 1/2-inch cubes. Cook in boiling, salted water for 3 to 5 minutes and drain well. Add the clams and juice, cracker crumbs, butter, onion powder, salt, pepper and corn and mix well. Stir in beaten egg yolks and fold in stiffly beaten egg whites. Pour into a casserole and sprinkle with cheese. Place casserole in pan of hot water. Bake at 350 degrees for 30 minutes. 6 servings.

Mrs. R. K. Jeffries, Alexandria, Louisiana

CLAM AND EGGPLANT CASSEROLE

1 lge. eggplant, pared	1/2 tsp. salt
Rind of 1/2 lemon	1/2 c. milk
3 tbsp. minced onion	2 7-oz. cans minced clams
1/4 c. chopped celery	1 egg, beaten
6 tbsp. butter or margarine	1 c. soft bread crumbs
1/4 c. flour	2 tbsp. Parmesan cheese

Preheat oven to 375 degrees. Cook eggplant in large saucepan in boiling water with lemon rind until partially done. Drain and discard lemon rind. Mash the eggplant. Saute the onion and celery in 1/4 cup butter in a medium saucepan until soft but not brown. Add the flour and salt and stir until smooth. Remove from heat. Add the milk gradually. Add the clams and clam juice and cook over medium heat, stirring constantly, until thickened. Stir in egg and eggplant and pour into a greased baking dish. Toss bread crumbs with remaining butter and sprinkle over eggplant mixture. Sprinkle with cheese. Bake for 25 minutes or until bread crumbs are light brown. 4 servings.

Maye Mefford, Longview, Texas

BAKED CRAB

2 tbsp. butter	2 tbsp. mayonnaise
2 tbsp. flour	1 lb. flaked crab meat
1 c. milk	1 c. bread or cracker crumbs
Salt and pepper to taste	

Melt the butter in a saucepan and stir in the flour. Add the milk and cook, stirring constantly, until thickened. Remove from heat and season with salt and pepper. Stir in mayonnaise and crab meat. Place in a casserole and cover with bread crumbs. Dot with additional butter. Bake at 350 degrees until heated through.

Mrs. Charles Martin Peery, New Market, Virginia

CRAB IMPERIAL

1 stick butter	Salt and pepper to taste
2 tbsp. flour	Red pepper to taste
1 c. milk	Worcestershire sauce to taste
2 tbsp. lemon juice	1 lb. back fin crab meat
1 tbsp. parsley flakes	1 c. crushed potato chips

Melt the butter in a saucepan. Add the flour and stir until smooth. Add the milk and cook, stirring, until thickened. Remove from heat. Season with lemon juice, parsley flakes, salt, pepper, red pepper and Worcestershire sauce. Add the crab meat and mix thoroughly. Place in a casserole or individual baking dishes and top with potato chip crumbs. Bake at 350 degrees until heated through and brown.

Mrs. V. G. Stewart, Wilson, North Carolina

CRAB CREOLE CASSEROLE

1 med. onion, finely chopped	Dash of thyme leaves
1 tbsp. butter	Dash of mace
2 tbsp. flour	2 tsp. Worcestershire sauce
4 med. tomatoes	2 c. cooked crab meat
1/4 c. chopped green olives	1 c. buttered bread crumbs
Salt and pepper to taste	

Cook the onion in butter in a saucepan for 2 minutes, stirring constantly. Add the flour and cook until light brown, stirring constantly. Peel and chop the tomatoes and add to sauce. Add the olives and mix thoroughly. Season with salt, pepper, thyme and mace. Simmer for 10 minutes and stir in Worcestershire sauce and crab meat. Place in a greased casserole and sprinkle with bread crumbs. Bake in 350-degree oven for 15 to 20 minutes or until crumbs are browned.

Julia Dehan, Shreveport, Louisiana

CRAB MEAT ST. JACQUES

1/4 onion, chopped	Paprika
1/2 green pepper, chopped	1 tsp. Worcestershire sauce
1/2 c. chopped mushrooms	1 lb. canned crab meat
Butter	1/2 c. grated American cheese
2 c. white sauce	1/2 c. buttered bread crumbs
Salt and pepper to taste	

Saute the onion, green pepper and mushrooms in a small amount of butter in a saucepan until tender. Add the white sauce, salt, pepper, 1/2 teaspoon paprika and Worcestershire sauce. Add crab meat and stir to mix. Place in a greased casserole and sprinkle with cheese, bread crumbs and paprika. Bake at 450 degrees for 15 minutes.

Mrs. John A. Bracey, Springfield, Tennessee

CRAB CASSEROLE

1 lb. Alaskan King crab	1 tbsp. minced onion
1 c. half and half	2 tbsp. chopped parsley
1 c. mayonnaise	1/2 c. grated sharp cheese
1 1/2 c. soft bread crumbs	1 c. corn flake crumbs
6 hard-boiled eggs, chopped	

Cut the crab in large pieces. Add the half and half, mayonnaise, bread crumbs, eggs, onion, parsley and 1/4 cup cheese and mix well. Place in a greased casserole. Place corn flake crumbs on top and sprinkle with remaining cheese. Bake in 350-degree oven for 45 minutes to 1 hour.

Mrs. W. H. Kuhrt, St. Petersburg, Florida

CASSEROLE WITH CRAB MEAT

2 7 3/4-oz. cans crab meat	1 3-oz. can cashews,
1 can mushroom soup	chopped fine
1/2 c. chopped onion	1 med. can chow mein noodles
1 c. chopped celery	1/3 c. cream

Combine all ingredients and mix well. Place in a casserole. Bake at 325 degrees for 30 minutes. 8 servings.

Mrs. Paul A. Lindig, Avondale Estates, Georgia

CRAB MEAT AND SPINACH CASSEROLE

4 tbsp. butter or margarine	1/2 tsp. monosodium glutamate
1/4 c. chopped onion	1 6-oz. can sliced mushrooms
2 cans cream of mushroom soup	2 7-oz. cans crab meat
1 c. sour cream	2 tbsp. sherry
1/2 c. grated Parmesan cheese	1 tbsp. chopped chives or
Dash of angostura bitters	parsley
1/2 tsp. dry mustard	1/2 lb. cooked spinach

Melt the butter in a saucepan and saute the onion in butter until tender. Add the soup, sour cream, cheese, bitters, mustard, monosodium glutamate and mushrooms and liquid and mix well. Cook until heated thoroughly. Drain and flake the crab meat and add to soup mixture. Stir in the sherry and chives. Place alternate layers of crab mixture and spinach in a baking dish. Bake at 350 degrees for 20 minutes and serve immediately. 8 servings.

Mrs. Albert W. Schinz, Eglin AFB, Florida

CREPES WITH CRAB MEAT

2 med. onions, chopped	2 sm. cans chili peppers
1 clove of garlic,	2 eggs, beaten
minced	4 c. milk
2 tbsp. cooking oil	2 c. sifted flour
1 1/2 No. 2 cans tomatoes	2 c. cooked crab meat
Pinch of salt	1 1/2 c. sour cream
Dash of pepper	

Cook the onions and garlic in oil until tender. Add the tomatoes, salt and pepper and simmer until tomatoes are soft. Cut the chili peppers in strips and add to tomato mixture. Mix the eggs and milk in a bowl. Add the flour gradually and beat until smooth. Pour enough batter into a greased small skillet to just cover bottom. Cook over very low heat until brown. Turn and brown on other side. Repeat with remaining batter. Fill each crepe with tomato mixture and crab meat and roll up. Place in a baking dish and pour remaining tomato mixture over crepes. Spread sour cream over top. Bake in 300-degree oven until heated through. May be made ahead of time and frozen, adding sour cream just before baking.

Mrs. Frank Yturria, Brownsville, Texas

CRAB AND RICE IN SEASHELLS

1 6 1/2-oz. can crab meat	Dash of pepper
1 c. cooked rice	1 tbsp. minced parsley
2 hard-cooked eggs, chopped	2 tsp. finely chopped onion
3 tbsp. mayonnaise	1/3 c. evaporated milk
1/2 tsp. salt	1/2 c. shredded Cheddar
1/4 tsp. cayenne pepper	cheese

Flake the crab meat and add the rice and eggs. Add remaining ingredients except cheese and mix well. Pour into 8 greased shell-shaped ramekins or individual casseroles and sprinkle with cheese. Bake at 350 degrees for 25 minutes or until cheese is melted. 8 servings.

Mrs. Lloyd C. Emery, Paducah, Kentucky

CRAB VERONIQUE

1 c. rice	1/4 c. flour
1 vegetable bouillon cube	1/2 tsp. salt
1 1/4 c. hot water	1 2/3 c. evaporated milk
1/2 c. chopped celery	1 c. apple juice
1/4 c. chopped parsley	1 tbsp. lemon juice
2 7-oz. cans crab meat	1 c. halved seeded green
1/4 c. butter or margarine	grapes

Cook the rice according to package directions and drain. Dissolve the bouillon cube in hot water and pour over rice. Stir in the celery and parsley. Drain the crab meat, flake and remove bony tissue. Melt the butter in a saucepan and stir in flour and salt. Add the milk and cook, stirring constantly, until thickened. Cook for 1 minute and remove from heat. Stir in apple juice and lemon juice and fold in crab meat and grapes. Place the rice mixture in a greased casserole or 6 individual greased baking dishes and spoon crab mixture over rice mixture. Bake at 375 degrees for 20 minutes or until bubbly and garnish with lemon slices. 6 servings.

Mrs. A. F. Groeneman, Miami, Oklahoma

LOBSTER-ARTICHOKE CASSEROLE

2 9-oz. packages frozen artichokes	2 cans cream of mushroom soup
Seasoned salt to taste	2 soup cans water
2 4 1/2-oz. packages precooked rice	American process cheese triangles
3 5-oz. cans lobster	Chopped parsley or chives

Place the artichokes in a 3-quart casserole and sprinkle with seasoned salt and rice. Drain the lobster and remove membrane. Place over rice. Blend the mushroom soup with water and pour over lobster. Bake at 400 degrees for 40 minutes or until bubbly. Top with cheese and sprinkle with parsley.

Mrs. Raymond Miles, Headland, Alabama

LOBSTER CASSEROLE SUPREME

1/2 c. butter	5 c. chopped lobster
1 c. flour	2/3 c. chopped ripe olives
1 1/2 tsp. salt	1 8-oz. can sliced mushrooms
8 c. milk	8 hard-cooked eggs, sliced
4 c. shredded Cheddar cheese	3 c. prepared biscuit mix

Melt the butter in a large saucepan and remove from heat. Stir in the flour and salt until smooth. Add 7 cups milk gradually and blend well. Cook and stir over low heat until thickened. Stir in 2 cups cheese and cook until melted. Add the lobster, olives, mushrooms and eggs and place in a 2-quart casserole. Add remaining milk to biscuit mix and mix well. Roll out on a floured surface into a rectangle 1/4 inch thick and cover with remaining cheese. Roll as for jelly roll and cut in 1/2-inch slices. Place over lobster mixture. Bake at 425 degrees for 15 minutes or until biscuits are browned. 16 servings.

Phyllis J. Hill, Phoenix, Arizona

BEST SCALLOPED OYSTERS

1 pt. oysters	2 tbsp. sherry
1 c. cracker crumbs	Dash of cayenne pepper
1/2 c. toast crumbs	1/2 tsp. salt
1/2 c. melted butter	1/4 tsp. pepper
1/4 c. cream	2 tbsp. butter
1 tsp. Worcestershire sauce	Paprika

Drain the oysters and reserve liquid. Toss cracker and toast crumbs with melted butter. Place 1/3 of the crumbs in a greased baking dish and top with 1/2 of the oysters. Mix reserved oyster liquid with cream, Worcestershire sauce, sherry, cayenne pepper, salt and pepper and pour 1/2 of the mixture over oysters. Cover with half the remaining crumbs, remaining oysters and remaining cream mixture. Top with remaining crumbs and dot with butter. Sprinkle with paprika. Bake at 400 degrees for 20 minutes. 8 servings.

Mrs. W. P. Bryant, Springfield, Tennessee

MINCED OYSTERS

3 pt. oysters and liquid	3/4 c. diced celery
4 slices dry toasted bread, crumbled	2 tbsp. chopped parsley
4 onions, finely chopped	Bacon drippings
1/2 green pepper, finely chopped	Salt and pepper to taste
	Juice of 1/2 lemon
	1 c. buttered bread crumbs

Chop the oysters and mix with dry bread crumbs. Saute the onions, green pepper, celery and parsley in small amount of bacon drippings in a saucepan until tender and add oyster mixture. Season with salt and pepper and stir in lemon juice. Cook until thickened. Pour into a greased baking dish and top with buttered bread crumbs. Bake at 350 degrees until browned. 6 servings.

Mrs. W. B. Franklin, LaGrange, Tennessee

DEVILED EGG AND SHRIMP CASSEROLE

6 hard-boiled eggs	1 c. cooked mushrooms
Mayonnaise to taste	2 tbsp. margarine
Mustard to taste	2 tbsp. flour
Salt and pepper to taste	1 c. milk
1 c. cooked shrimp	1/2 c. grated cheese

Cut the eggs in half crosswise and remove yolks. Mash egg yolks and mix with mayonnaise, mustard, salt and pepper. Fill egg whites with yolk mixture and place in a casserole. Add shrimp and mushrooms. Melt the margarine in a saucepan and blend in flour. Add the milk and cook over low heat until thickened, stirring constantly. Add the cheese and heat until melted. Pour over shrimp mixture. Bake at 350 degrees for 15 minutes.

Mrs. J. D. Moore, Cameron, Texas

CHEESE-SHRIMP CASSEROLE

1/3 c. vegetable shortening	1 c. diced American process
1/2 c. chopped green pepper	cheese
2 c. shrimp	1/4 c. sliced canned pimento
1/4 c. flour	2 tbsp. chopped parsley
2 tsp. salt	3 c. cooked rice
1/4 tsp. oregano	Parsley sprigs
2 c. milk	

Place the shortening in a skillet and place skillet over low heat. Add the green pepper and cook until tender. Reserve several whole shrimp for garnish. Cut remaining shrimp in 1-inch pieces and add to green pepper. Stir until shrimp turn pink, then stir in flour, salt and oregano. Add milk gradually and bring to a boil, stirring constantly. Cook for 1 minute. Add cheese and pimento and stir until cheese melts. Remove from heat. Mix chopped parsley and rice and spread in a greased 2-quart casserole. Pour shrimp mixture over rice and place reserved shrimp on top. Bake in 325-degree oven for 25 to 30 minutes or until bubbly and garnish with parsley sprigs. 6 servings.

Cheese-Shrimp Casserole (above)

CHARLESTON SHRIMP CASSEROLE

2 lb. cooked shrimp, cleaned	3 tbsp. butter
2 c. bread crumbs	1 tbsp. hot sauce
2 c. tomato juice	2 tbsp. Worcestershire sauce
1/2 tsp. salt	1 c. catsup

Combine all ingredients and pour into a casserole. Bake at 350 degrees for 30 minutes. 8 servings.

Mrs. J. C. Reid, Charleston, South Carolina

FILLET OF SOLE AND SHRIMP CASSEROLE

3 lb. fillet of sole	Milk
2 1/2 tsp. salt	1 tbsp. grated onion
1/4 tsp. pepper	1/8 tsp. cayenne pepper
1/4 tsp. paprika	1/2 lb. grated Parmesan
2 cans mushrooms	cheese
6 tbsp. butter or margarine	1 1/2 lb. cooked shrimp
5 tbsp. flour	

Cut sole into serving pieces and saute in a skillet for 1 minute on each side. Place in a baking dish and sprinkle with salt, pepper and paprika. Drain the mushrooms and reserve liquid and 12 mushrooms. Melt the butter in a double boiler and stir in flour. Mix reserved mushroom liquid with enough milk to make 2 cups liquid and stir into flour mixture. Cook, stirring, until thickened, then stir in onion and cayenne pepper. Add the cheese and stir until melted. Reserve 12 shrimp. Add remaining shrimp to cheese sauce and heat through. Pour over sole and garnish with reserved mushrooms and shrimp. Bake at 350 degrees for 30 minutes. 8 servings.

Mrs. George B. Eyerly, Malvern, Arkansas

SEAFOOD LOUISIANA

1/2 c. chopped onion	Dash of cayenne pepper
1 clove of garlic, minced	1/2 tsp. chili powder
1/4 c. chopped green pepper	2 tbsp. grated Parmesan cheese
1/4 c. butter or margarine	1/2 tsp. sugar
2 tbsp. flour	1 pt. scallops
1 No. 2 1/2 can tomatoes	1 pt. oysters
1 1/2 tsp. salt	3 c. hot cooked rice
Dash of pepper	

Saute the onion, garlic and green pepper in butter in a saucepan until light brown and stir in flour. Add the tomatoes, salt, pepper, cayenne pepper, chili powder, cheese, sugar, scallops and oysters and mix well. Place the rice in a casserole and pour scallop mixture over rice. Bake at 325 degrees for 15 minutes. 4-6 servings.

Mrs. Earl Le Moine, Monongah, West Virginia

lamb, variety meats, and game

When you want to add new sparkle to your lunch and dinner menus, turn to lamb, variety meats, and game. These meats bring bright new flavors to your every meal. For even more flavor notes, try adding your favorite sauce!

Lamb is rapidly gaining popularity with southern homemakers who enjoy its mild flavor — especially in such classic dishes as spicy-hot Lamb Pilaf. The recipe for this traditional Mediterranean favorite, with some brand new touches added by a clever southern cook, is in the section that follows. So is another homemaker's favorite recipe for Yorkshire Hotchpot, a sure-to-satisfy combination of lamb chops, onions, potatoes, and beans.

Another long-time southern favorite is the variety meats. Homemakers throughout the Southland appreciate their low cost and high nutritional values. In this section, the very best variety meat casserole recipes have been brought together for your dining pleasure . . . recipes like Liver and Onions and Corned Beef and Green Beans.

And when your favorite hunters return from the fields flushed with their success, this is the section where you'll find such delectable recipes as Dove Pie and Wild Duck Casserole.

Yes, the next time you want to treat your family and guests to something brand new, this is the section for you!

Mexican Lamb Chops (below)

MEXICAN LAMB CHOPS

4 shoulder lamb chops, 1 in.
   thick
Seasoned flour
3 tbsp. butter or margarine
1 8 1/2-oz. can pineapple
   slices, drained
3/4 c. orange juice
1/4 c. lemon juice
2/3 c. dry white wine

1/2 c. dark seedless raisins
2 tbsp. light brown sugar
1/4 tsp. cinnamon
1/4 tsp. nutmeg
2 med. green-tipped bananas,
   cut in chunks
1/2 c. slivered toasted
   almonds
Hot cooked rice

Dredge the lamb chops with seasoned flour. Cook in butter in a skillet until brown on both sides and place in a shallow baking dish. Top each chop with 1 pineapple slice. Combine the orange juice, lemon juice, wine, raisins, sugar and spices and pour over chops. Bake in 350-degree oven for 40 minutes or until chops are tender. Add bananas and almonds and bake for 5 minutes longer. Serve with rice. 4 servings.

SCALLOPED POTATOES AND LAMB

4 c. sliced pared potatoes
2/3 c. minced onions
2 tbsp. flour
1 tsp. salt
1/8 tsp. pepper

2 tbsp. butter or margarine
6 lamb chops
1 1/2 c. scalded milk
Paprika to taste

Place half the potatoes in a greased 2-quart casserole and cover with half the onions. Mix the flour, salt and pepper and sprinkle half the mixture on onions. Dot with half the butter. Repeat layers and top with lamb chops. Pour milk over casserole and sprinkle with paprika. Cover. Bake at 350 degrees for 1 hour and 30 minutes.

Mrs. Peter Von Wiese, Birmingham, Alabama

DINNER FOR SIX

1 lb. small white onions	3 lge. baking apples
12 loin lamb chops, 3/4 in. thick	Juice of 1/2 lemon
	1 lb. cooked sm. whole carrots
Onion salt to taste	1 10-oz. jar currant jelly

Cook the onions in boiling, salted water until almost tender. Sprinkle the lamb chops with onion salt and brown on both sides in a large skillet in small amount of fat. Peel the apples and cut in half. Remove cores and sprinkle apples with lemon juice. Stand 10 chops around sides of shallow casserole and place remaining chops on bottom. Arrange apples around casserole and place onions over chops on bottom of casserole. Arrange carrots around and between chops and apples. Melt the jelly and spoon half the jelly over casserole. Cover with plastic wrap and refrigerate until chilled. Bake in 350-degree oven for 15 minutes. Brush all ingredients with remaining jelly and bake for 15 minutes longer or until apples are tender.

Mrs. David Baker, Naples, Florida

LAMB CHOPS WITH SPINACH DRESSING

1 med. onion, minced	4 1/2 c. chopped spinach
1 tbsp. fat	4 1/2 c. fine soft bread crumbs
6 lamb shoulder chops	2 eggs
2 tsp. salt	Celery salt to taste

Saute the onion in fat in a skillet until soft and remove from skillet. Season the lamb chops with 1/2 teaspoon salt and brown in the skillet on both sides. Mix the spinach, bread crumbs, onion, eggs, remaining salt and celery salt and blend well. Place in a shallow baking dish and top with lamb chops. Cover. Bake at 350 degrees for 1 hour or until chops are tender.

Mrs. William B. Marks, Harrisonburg, Virginia

LAMB CHOPS WITH DRESSING

5 lamb shoulder chops	1/2 to 1 tsp. poultry seasoning
2 tbsp. bacon fat	1/2 tsp. salt
3 c. coarse bread crumbs	1 egg, beaten
1/2 c. cold water	5 slices bacon, partially cooked
1 med. onion, grated	
2 tbsp. chopped parsley	

Brown the lamb chops in fat in a skillet. Soak crumbs in water until all water is absorbed and squeeze out excess water. Sprinkle the onion, parsley and seasonings over crumbs. Add the egg and mix well. Place in a buttered baking dish and cover with lamb chops. Cover. Bake at 350 degrees for about 1 hour. Remove cover and place 1 slice bacon on each chop. Bake for 15 minutes longer or until bacon is crisp. 5 servings.

Mrs. Marie Booth, Old Town, Florida

YORKSHIRE HOTCHPOT

4 lamb shoulder chops	2 tsp. salt
1 clove of garlic, mashed	1/8 tsp. pepper
4 sm. white onions	1 can cream of mushroom soup
4 med. potatoes, pared and halved	1/2 soup can water
	Paprika to taste
1 pkg. frozen cut green beans	1 tbsp. chopped parsley

Cut the fat from lamb chops and brown chops on both sides in heavy skillet. Place in a large, shallow casserole. Add the garlic, onions, potatoes and beans and season with salt and pepper. Mix the soup and water and pour over bean mixture. Cover. Bake in 375-degree oven for 1 hour and sprinkle with paprika and parsley just before serving. 4 servings.

Mrs. T. O. Vinson, Dover, Delaware

BAKED LAMB WITH CORNMEAL BISCUITS

1 1/2 lb. cubed lamb shoulder	3 c. stock or bouillon
1 c. sliced onions	Salt and pepper to taste
1 1/2 c. sliced beets	1 1/2 c. prepared biscuit mix
1 1/2 c. cut green beans	1/2 c. yellow cornmeal
2 c. diced tomatoes	1/2 c. milk
1 c. sliced mushrooms	

Place the lamb and onions in a skillet and cook over low heat until lamb is browned. Add the beets, green beans, tomatoes, mushrooms, stock and seasonings and mix well. Turn into a 3-quart casserole and cover. Bake at 350 degrees for 1 hour. Combine the biscuit mix and cornmeal in a bowl. Add the milk and mix lightly. Turn onto lightly floured surface and knead 10 times. Roll out 1/2 inch thick and cut with a floured biscuit cutter. Place over stew. Increase the temperature to 400 degrees and bake for 15 minutes longer or until biscuits are browned. 6 servings.

Mrs. Lou Massey, Camden, Arkansas

CABBAGE ROLLS WITH LAMB

1 med. cabbage	1/8 tsp. pepper
3 lamb chops, cut in cubes	1/2 c. canned tomatoes
1 c. rice	Garlic to taste
Salt	

Separate cabbage leaves and cook in boiling water until tender. Cut into quarters. Combine the lamb, rice, salt to taste, pepper and tomatoes. Place 1 teaspoon lamb mixture in each cabbage leaf quarter and roll. Place rolls close together in baking dish and add garlic. Pour 1 cup water and 1 tablespoon salt over rolls and cover. Bake at 300 degrees for 1 hour. 5-6 servings.

Mrs. Daniel Ray, Shreveport, Louisiana

DUBLIN LAMB STEW

4 lb. breast or lean shoulder of lamb	1 stalk celery, diced
6 med. onions, sliced	Salt and pepper to taste
6 med. potatoes, peeled and sliced	3 sprigs of parsley
	1 bay leaf

Cut the lamb in small cubes. Place 1/3 of the lamb in a large casserole and add half the onions. Add half the potatoes and celery and season with salt and pepper. Repeat layers, ending with lamb. Add the parsley and bay leaf, then add just enough water to cover. Cover the casserole. Bake at 350 degrees for 1 hour and 30 minutes or until lamb is tender. 6 servings.

Mrs. Stewart Fleming, Mobile, Alabama

LAMB SAN GABRIEL

2 lb. lamb shoulder	1 4-oz. jar pimento
1/4 c. flour	1 med. green pepper
3 tbsp. salad oil	1 tsp. salt
1 med. onion, sliced	1/2 tsp. pepper
1 c. stock or bouillon	1/2 tsp. crushed basil
1 1/2 c. cooked pinto beans	1/2 tsp. crushed thyme
1 can whole kernel corn	

Cut the lamb in cubes and coat with flour. Brown on all sides in oil in a large skillet and remove from skillet. Add onion to skillet and cook until golden. Stir in the stock, beans and corn. Drain the pimento and chop. Add to corn mixture. Cut the green pepper in strips and add to corn mixture. Add remaining ingredients and lamb and mix well. Place in a lightly greased 2-quart casserole and cover. Bake at 350 degrees for 1 hour or until lamb is tender. 6 servings.

Lamb San Gabriel (above)

125

COMPANY CASSEROLE

3 tbsp. salad oil	1/8 tsp. pepper
2 c. diced pared eggplant	1 1-lb. can tomatoes
2 tbsp. instant minced onion	Bouquet garni for lamb
1 tbsp. minced green pepper	1/8 tsp. grated lemon rind
1/4 c. water	1 c. cooked brown rice or
2 c. lamb, cut in 1/2-in. cubes	cracked wheat
1/4 tsp. garlic powder	1/4 c. grated Parmesan or
2 tsp. Beau Monde seasoning	Romano cheese
1 tsp. salt	

Heat the oil in a heavy frying pan. Add the eggplant and cover. Cook over low heat until almost tender. Add the onion, green pepper, water and lamb and cook until onion and lamb are lightly browned. Add the garlic powder, Beau Monde seasoning, salt and pepper. Stir in tomatoes and add bouquet garni and lemon rind. Simmer for about 20 minutes. Spoon rice into a 1 1/2-quart casserole and top with lamb mixture. Sprinkle with cheese. Bake at 375 degrees until browned and bubbly. Remove bouquet garni and serve. 6 servings.

Mrs. James Bunche, Smyrna, Georgia

LAMB AND BROWN RICE

1 1/2 lb. boned lamb shoulder	1 qt. water
6 tbsp. flour	1 tsp. Worcestershire sauce
1/4 c. salad oil	1 tsp. salt
2/3 c. brown rice	1/2 tsp. thyme
1 sm. onion, sliced	1/8 tsp. pepper

Cut the lamb in 1-inch squares and dredge with 4 tablespoons flour. Heat the oil in a large skillet. Add the lamb and cook until brown. Place the rice in a casserole and cover with lamb and onion. Place remaining flour in the skillet and cook until brown. Add the water and seasonings and blend well. Pour over lamb mixture and cover. Bake at 375 degrees for 2 hours, adding water, if necessary. 6 servings.

Mrs. Eloise Preston, Mexico Beach, Florida

LAMB WITH SHERRY

2 c. diced cooked lamb	1 7-oz. can mushrooms,
2 onions, sliced	drained
3 med. potatoes, sliced	1 c. gravy
1 10-oz. can peas	Paprika to taste
3 tbsp. dry sherry	

Place alternate layers of the lamb, onions, potatoes and peas in a greased 2-quart baking dish. Pour the sherry, mushrooms and gravy over top and sprinkle with paprika. Cover. Bake at 350 degrees for 1 hour and 15 minutes. Uncover and bake for 15 minutes longer. 6 servings.

Mrs. Jerome Hartley, Columbia, South Carolina

LAMB WITH MUSHROOMS

2 lb. lamb shoulder, cut in cubes	3/4 c. meat or mushroom stock
2 tsp. chopped onion	Salt and pepper to taste
2 tbsp. bacon fat	1 c. tomatoes
2 tbsp. flour	1 c. mushrooms
	Chopped parsley to taste

Brown the lamb and onion in fat in a skillet and place in a casserole. Add flour to remaining fat in the skillet and cook, stirring, until browned. Add the meat stock and cook until thickened. Pour over the lamb and add seasonings, tomatoes and mushrooms. Cover. Bake at 350 degrees for 1 hour and sprinkle with parsley. 4 servings.

Mrs. Hellman Cole, Albuquerque, New Mexico

LAMB PILAF

2 lb. boned lamb, cut in cubes	3/4 c. chopped pitted prunes
4 tbsp. butter	2 c. cooked rice
3 med. onions, sliced	1 1/2 tbsp. melted butter
1/4 tsp. cinnamon	3 tbsp. lemon juice
1/4 tsp. pepper	1 tbsp. minced fresh parsley
1 tsp. salt	1/2 c. chopped almonds
1/2 c. raisins	

Cook the lamb in butter in a heavy skillet until brown. Add the onions, cinnamon, pepper and 2 cups water and cover. Cook for 2 hours and 30 minutes. Stir in the salt and cool. Cover the raisins with boiling water and let stand for 15 to 20 minutes. Drain. Drain the lamb and reserve liquid. Add the raisins and prunes to lamb and mix well. Place in a large casserole and cover with rice. Pour reserved liquid over rice and cover the casserole. Bake at 300 degrees for 35 to 40 minutes. Blend the butter and lemon juice and spoon over rice. Top with parsley and almonds. 6-8 servings.

Mrs. Chilton Powell, Oklahoma City, Oklahoma

POTATO-TOPPED CASSEROLE

2 tbsp. butter	Salt and pepper to taste
1 tsp. instant minced onion	2 c. diced cooked lamb
1 tsp. thyme	1 can beef gravy
1 tbsp. dried parsley flakes	2 c. mashed potatoes
1 c. sliced celery	Paprika to taste

Melt the butter in a saucepan. Add the onion, thyme, parsley and celery and cook over low heat for 5 minutes. Add the salt, pepper and lamb and stir well. Add the gravy and cook for 5 minutes. Pour into a casserole and top with potatoes. Dot with additional butter and sprinkle with paprika. Bake at 350 degrees until brown. 4-6 servings.

Mrs. Boykin B. Jordan, Annapolis, Maryland

LAMB AND EGGPLANT

2 eggplant
2 1/4 c. ground lamb
1/4 c. butter
Salt and pepper to taste
1/3 c. cream
2 eggs, beaten

1/4 tsp. thyme
1/4 tsp. rosemary
1 sm. can mushrooms, drained
1/2 c. bread crumbs
1/2 c. grated cheese

Peel and cube the eggplant. Cook in boiling, salted water until tender, then drain and mash. Saute the lamb in 2 tablespoons butter until brown and season with salt and pepper. Mix the cream, eggs, thyme and rosemary and stir in the mushrooms, eggplant and lamb. Pour into a 1-quart casserole and cover with bread crumbs. Dot with remaining butter and sprinkle with cheese. Bake at 350 degrees for 20 to 30 minutes. 6-8 servings.

Mary S. Briscoe, Prince Frederick, Maryland

MOUSSAKA CASSEROLE

2 1/2 lb. eggplant
Salt
1 sm. onion, chopped
2 tbsp. fat
2 lb. ground lamb
1 tsp. paprika

1/4 tsp. pepper
Flour
3 med. tomatoes, sliced
1/2 pt. yogurt
4 egg yolks

Peel the eggplant and cut in 1/4-inch slices. Sprinkle with salt to taste and let stand for 1 hour. Saute the onion in fat in a skillet until tender. Add the lamb, 2 teaspoons salt, paprika and pepper and cook until brown. Drain and reserve fat. Dip eggplant slices into flour and brown in reserved fat. Place alternate layers of lamb mixture and eggplant in a 3-quart casserole and top with tomato slices. Bake at 350 degrees for 1 hour. Combine the yogurt, egg yolks and 1/2 cup sifted flour and mix well. Pour over casserole. Bake for 15 minutes longer or until brown.

Mrs. Anna Elizabeth Davis, Springdale, Arkansas

RICE RANCHERO

2 cans chili-beef soup
1 1/2 c. water
1 med. onion, chopped
1 1/4 c. precooked rice

1 c. shredded sharp Cheddar
  cheese
1 c. crushed corn chips

Combine the soup, water and onion in a medium saucepan and bring to boiling point, stirring occasionally. Add the rice and pour into a 2-quart casserole. Cover. Bake at 375 degrees for 30 minutes. Uncover and fluff rice with a fork. Top with cheese and bake for 10 minutes longer. Add the corn chips just before serving. 6-8 servings.

Susan Toaz, Bradenton, Florida

CORNED BEEF HAWAIIAN

1 can sweet potatoes	1 tsp. vanilla
1/4 c. orange juice	1 tbsp. cornstarch
1/4 c. brown sugar	1 can corned beef

Drain the sweet potatoes and reserve liquid. Mix reserved liquid, orange juice, brown sugar, vanilla and cornstarch. Place corned beef in center of a greased casserole and arrange sweet potatoes around corned beef. Pour orange juice mixture over potatoes and corned beef. Bake at 350 degrees until done. 4 servings.

Mrs. Ann P. Jeter, Crestview, Florida

CORNED BEEF WITH GREEN BEANS

6 hard-cooked eggs	2 c. milk
1/4 c. mayonnaise	1 c. grated Cheddar cheese
1/2 tsp. salt	1 1-lb. can cut green beans
Dash of pepper	1 12-oz. can corned beef,
1/4 tsp. Worcestershire sauce	flaked
1/4 c. melted margarine	Buttered strips of bread
1/4 c. flour	

Cut the eggs in half lengthwise. Remove yolks and mash. Add the mayonnaise, salt, pepper and Worcestershire sauce and mix well. Fill egg whites and place in a casserole. Blend margarine and flour in a saucepan and stir in milk gradually. Cook until thickened, stirring constantly, and stir in the cheese. Drain the beans and add to cheese sauce. Flake the corned beef and stir into cheese sauce. Pour over eggs and overlap bread strips around edge of casserole. Bake at 350 degrees for 15 to 20 minutes.

Mrs. Hollis Jones, Liberty, Mississippi

CORNED BEEF LASAGNA

1 8-oz. package lasagna	1/4 tsp. basil
2 12-oz. cans corned beef	1 c. cottage cheese
2 tbsp. butter or margarine	1 8-oz. package cream cheese
1 1-lb. can tomatoes	1/2 c. sour cream
1 8-oz. can tomato sauce	1/3 c. chopped green onions
1/4 tsp. oregano	6 oz. sliced mozzarella cheese

Cook the lasagna according to package directions and drain. Flake the corned beef and heat in butter in a saucepan. Add the tomatoes, tomato sauce, oregano and basil. Mix the cottage cheese, cream cheese and sour cream and stir in the onions. Place half the lasagna in a greased 2 1/2-quart casserole and add half the corned beef mixture. Add half the cheese mixture. Repeat layers and top with mozzarella cheese. Bake at 350 degrees for 30 minutes. 8-10 servings.

Mrs. Morgan Smith, Dallas, Texas

Pancake Supper with Chipped Beef (below)

PANCAKE SUPPER WITH CHIPPED BEEF

4 eggs, well beaten	4 tbsp. butter
1 c. cottage cheese, sieved	Dash of pepper
1/2 tsp. salt	2 2 1/2-oz. jars chipped
1 c. instant nonfat dry milk	beef
Flour	Grated Parmesan cheese
24 sm. cooked asparagus spears	

Mix the eggs and cottage cheese in a mixing bowl. Add the salt, 1/3 cup milk, 1/3 cup sifted flour and 2 tablespoons water and mix well. Drop batter, 1/4 cup at a time, on hot, greased griddle and cook until golden brown. Turn and cook until brown. Roll each pancake around 3 asparagus spears and place side by side in a shallow casserole. Melt the butter in a saucepan, remove from heat and blend in 4 tablespoons flour. Mix remaining milk, pepper and 2 cups water, add to flour mixture and stir until mixed. Cook over low heat until thickened, stirring constantly. Add the chipped beef and mix well. Pour over rolled pancakes in casserole and sprinkle with desired amount of Parmesan cheese. Bake at 350 degrees for 20 to 25 minutes. 8 servings.

DRIED BEEF AU GRATIN

1/2 pkg. egg noodles	1/2 c. sliced mushrooms
6 tbsp. butter	5 oz. chipped beef
3 tbsp. flour	2 tbsp. minced pimento
1 1/2 c. milk	1/4 tsp. pepper
1/4 lb. Cheddar cheese, grated	1/3 c. buttered bread crumbs

Cook the noodles according to package directions and drain. Melt 2 tablespoons butter in a saucepan and stir in the flour. Add the milk and cook, stirring constantly, until thickened. Add the cheese and stir until melted. Remove from heat. Saute the mushrooms in remaining butter in a saucepan until tender and add to sauce. Saute the chipped beef in butter remaining in saucepan until edges curl. Add the sauce, noodles, pimento and pepper. Place in a casserole and top with crumbs. Bake at 375 degrees for 30 minutes. 4-6 servings.

Joyce J. Terrass, Wichita, Kansas

BARGAIN PORK AND BEANS SKILLET

1 12-oz. can luncheon meat	1 can pork and beans with
2 tbsp. butter or margarine	tomato sauce
1/2 c. mincemeat	4 orange slices (opt.)

Cut the luncheon meat in thin strips and brown in the butter in a skillet. Add the pork and beans and mincemeat and mix. Bake at 350 degrees until heated through. Garnish with orange slices. 4 servings.

Photograph for this recipe on page 120.

FRANKLY CORNY STRATA

6 slices day-old bread	1/2 tsp. salt
6 frankfurters	1/2 c. milk
4 slices pimento cheese,	1 17-oz. can yellow
quartered	cream-style corn
2 eggs, slightly beaten	

Cut the bread in 1/2-inch cubes and place half the bread in a greased 8-inch square casserole. Slice the frankfurters and place over the bread. Add the cheese and cover with remaining bread cubes. Mix the eggs, salt, milk and corn and pour over bread. Let stand for 10 minutes. Bake at 375 degrees for about 25 minutes. 4-6 servings.

Audrey Mathis, Gastonia, North Carolina

FRANKFURTERS WITH CABBAGE WEDGES

1 lge. cabbage	2 c. milk
1 1/2 tsp. salt	1/4 c. sweet pickle relish
1/4 c. butter or margarine	3 tbsp. prepared mustard
1/3 c. chopped onion	1 lb. frankfurters
1/4 c. flour	

Cut cabbage into 6 wedges and place in a saucepan. Add enough water to cover and cook for 5 minutes. Drain. Place in a 2-quart casserole and sprinkle with 1/2 teaspoon salt. Melt the butter in a saucepan. Add the onion and cook until soft. Blend in flour and remaining salt. Add the milk and cook until thick and smooth, stirring constantly. Stir in pickle relish and mustard and pour over cabbage. Cut the frankfurters in half crosswise and place between cabbage wedges. Bake at 350 degrees for about 20 minutes. 6 servings.

Mrs. Lector Thomason, Rochester, Texas

LIVER AND ONIONS AU GRATIN

3/4 c. flour	12 sm. onions
2 tbsp. salt	1/2 c. grated sharp cheese
1 1/2 lb. sliced beef liver	1 1/2 c. medium white sauce
1/2 c. bacon fat	1 1/2 c. buttered bread crumbs

Mix the flour and salt and dredge liver with flour mixture. Place bacon fat in a baking pan and place liver in fat, turning to coat both sides. Bake at 400 degrees for 15 to 20 minutes or until light brown. Cook the onions in boiling, salted water for 15 minutes and drain. Place on liver. Add cheese to white sauce and pour over onions. Sprinkle with crumbs. Bake for 10 to 15 minutes longer or until crumbs are brown. 6 servings.

Mrs. G. H. Renell, Murrells Inlet, South Carolina

SCALLOPED POTATOES WITH SALAMI SLICES

1/4 c. butter	3 c. milk
1/4 c. flour	1/2 lb. thinly sliced salami
1/2 tsp. salt	4 c. thinly sliced potatoes
1/4 tsp. pepper	1 med. onion, thinly sliced

Melt the butter in a saucepan over low heat and blend in flour and seasonings. Add the milk slowly and cook, stirring constantly, until smooth and thickened. Cut the salami slices in quarters. Arrange alternate layers of potatoes, onion, salami and white sauce in a greased 2-quart casserole and cover the casserole. Bake at 350 degrees for 40 minutes. Remove cover and bake for 20 to 30 minutes longer or until potatoes are tender and top is brown. 6 servings.

Scalloped Potatoes with Salami Slices (above)

LUNCHEON MEAT-BROCCOLI DISH

2 12-oz. cans luncheon meat	2 c. mashed potatoes
Prepared mustard	2 tbsp. margarine
2 pkg. frozen broccoli spears	

Cut each can of luncheon meat into 3 slices and place in a 2-quart baking dish. Spread with mustard. Thaw the broccoli and place over luncheon meat. Top with potatoes and dot with margarine. Bake in 350-degree oven for 35 minutes or until potatoes are brown. 6 servings.

Mrs. Josh E. Wright, Nathalie, Virginia

DOVE PIE

10 dove breasts	Flour
Tops and leaves of 6 stalks celery	4 tsp. baking powder
1 stick butter or margarine	2 eggs
Salt	Milk
Pepper to taste	1 recipe pastry

Place the dove breasts in a kettle and cover with water. Add the celery and bring to a boil. Reduce heat and simmer until dove breasts are tender. Remove dove and celery from the stock and add the margarine, salt to taste and pepper to stock. Sift 2 cups flour, baking powder and 1 teaspoon salt together 3 times and place in a bowl. Beat the eggs well and add enough milk to make 1 cup liquid. Stir into flour mixture, adding milk, if needed, as dough should be stiff. Thicken stock with flour mixed with water. Drop the dough from a wet spoon into the stock and cover. Simmer for 2 minutes. Line a baking dish with pastry and place dove breasts on pastry. Add dumplings and stock. Cover with pastry and cut slits in center of pastry. Bake at 350 degrees until brown.

Mrs. Avery Burdette, Guntersville, Alabama

WILD DUCK CASSEROLE

2 ducks	1 tbsp. chopped parsley
Seasoned flour	1/4 tsp. thyme
2 tsp. powdered ginger	1/4 tsp. marjoram
1/4 c. butter	1/4 tsp. basil
1/2 clove of garlic, minced	4 oz. dry white wine
1/2 lb. fresh mushrooms, sliced	1 tbsp. brandy
1 sm. green onion, chopped	1/2 c. cream

Cut ducks into serving pieces. Dredge with seasoned flour and sprinkle with ginger. Melt the butter in a heavy skillet and add garlic, mushrooms and ducks. Cook until brown and place in a casserole. Add remaining ingredients except cream and cover casserole. Bake at 350 degrees for 1 hour. Add the cream and bake for 25 to 30 minutes longer or until ducks are tender. 6 servings.

Mrs. McLean Smith, Dallas, Texas

Angostura Duckling Casserole (below)

ANGOSTURA DUCKLING CASSEROLE

1 5-lb. duckling	2 tsp. salt

2 tbsp. angostura aromatic
   bitters
	1 6-oz. can frozen concentrated
	   orange juice, thawed

1 1/2 c. brown rice	2 c. water or broth
1 6-oz. can sliced mushrooms	6 carrots, sliced
1 med. onion, chopped	1 green pepper, chopped
1/2 tsp. poultry seasoning	

Preheat oven to 350 degrees. Cut the duckling in serving pieces and brush with angostura bitters. Chop the duckling fat and fry in a large skillet until pieces are crisp. Remove crisp pieces and brown duckling in the fat on all sides. Cover and cook over low heat for 30 minutes. Pour rice into a greased 3-quart casserole and top with duckling. Spoon 1/4 cup duckling drippings in the skillet over duckling. Combine the mushrooms and liquid, onion, poultry seasoning, salt, orange juice and water and pour over duckling. Add the carrots and green pepper and cover. Bake for 40 to 50 minutes or until duckling and rice are tender. 6-8 servings.

DOVE IN SOUR CREAM

12 dove	4 slices bacon
Salt and pepper to taste	1 c. beef or chicken stock
Flour	1 c. sour cream
Oil or butter	

Wash and dry the dove and season with salt and pepper. Roll in flour and brown lightly in small amount of oil in a skillet. Place the bacon in a casserole and place the dove on bacon. Add the stock and cover. Bake at 350 degrees for 50 minutes. Uncover and pour sour cream over the dove. Bake 10 minutes longer.

Mrs. W. C. Lindley, Williams AFB, Arizona

PHEASANT WITH ASPARAGUS

3/4 c. butter	1 c. grated sharp cheese
1/2 c. flour	1 can pimento, chopped
4 c. milk	3 c. round buttery cracker
1/2 tsp. salt	crumbs
1/4 tsp. pepper	4 c. chopped cooked pheasant
4 hard-cooked eggs, chopped	1 can green asparagus

Melt 1/2 cup butter in a saucepan and blend in flour. Add the milk and seasonings and cook, stirring constantly, until thickened. Add eggs, cheese and pimento. Place 1 cup crumbs in a greased 2-quart casserole and add half the egg mixture. Add half the pheasant and half the asparagus. Repeat layers, ending with crumbs. Melt remaining butter and pour over crumbs. Bake at 350 degrees for 30 minutes or until browned. 10 servings.

Mrs. Robert Baron, Jackson, Mississippi

QUAIL CASSEROLE

4 quail	1 tbsp. minced green pepper
Salt to taste	3/4 c. sliced mushrooms
1/3 c. mixed salad oil and	2 tbsp. flour
butter	2 c. stock or bouillon
1 carrot, finely chopped	1/3 c. white wine
1 sm. onion, minced	

Season the quail with salt. Brown in oil mixture in a skillet and remove to a casserole. Saute the carrot, onion, green pepper and mushrooms in same skillet for 5 minutes. Blend in flour and stir in stock gradually. Season with salt and pour over quail. Add the wine and cover. Bake in 350-degree oven for about 30 minutes or until quail are tender. 4 servings.

Mrs. Thomas I. Vermillion, Farmville, Virginia

VENISON WITH SOUR CREAM

2 lb. venison	1 tsp. salt
1/4 c. fat	1 bay leaf
1 clove of garlic	2 c. water
1 c. diced celery	4 tbsp. butter
1/2 c. minced onion	4 tbsp. flour
1 c. diced carrots	1 c. sour cream

Cut the venison in serving pieces. Melt the fat in a heavy frying pan. Add the venison and garlic and brown well. Place in a baking dish. Cook the celery, onion and carrots in remaining fat in frying pan for 2 minutes. Add the salt, bay leaf and water and pour over venison. Bake at 300 degrees until venison is tender, then drain and reserve broth. Melt the butter in frying pan and stir in flour. Add reserved broth and cook until thick. Add sour cream and additional salt, if needed, and pour over venison mixture. Serve with buttered noodles. 4-6 servings.

Mrs. Uyvonna C. Bell, Eatonton, Georgia

combination meats

Looking for ways to vary your menus? Try combination meats! Every recipe in this section combines meats, vegetables, and fish into brand new taste treats. For example, everyone knows how delicious chicken and ham are on their own. But have you thought of combining them? One innovative homemaker did, and her favorite recipe for Chicken Dish Supreme mixes ham and chicken with mushrooms and cheese in an unforgettable flavor treat!

Another unusual dish — Shrimp with Pork and Chicken — mixes three popular flavors into a unique adventure in casserole dining.

These recipes are just a few of the exciting combinations you will find as you browse through this section. Many of the recipes have been especially developed by southern homemakers from the meats their families love best. Many others reflect the cuisine of far-away lands. Bammi is one such recipe. India-like in its curry flavor, Bammi combines ground pork and beef in a spicy-rich casserole certain to spark up any supper menu. From the cuisine of Mexico comes Montezuma Special, a hot, sweet combination of olives, beef, and sausage.

As you look over the recipes in the section that follows, remember that all have been home-tested with southern families. These are the family pleasers — try one and see!

CHICKEN DISH SUPREME

6 sm. chicken breasts	2 tbsp. flour
6 tbsp. melted butter	1 tbsp. salt
1/4 c. water	1/4 tsp. pepper
6 slices toast	2 c. light cream
6 slices ham	1 c. grated sharp cheese
1 4-oz. can mushrooms	1/2 tsp. Worcestershire sauce

Brown the chicken lightly in 3 tablespoons butter in a skillet and add water. Cover and simmer for 30 minutes. Cool and remove chicken from bones. Place toast in buttered shallow casserole and top with ham slices. Add chicken breasts and sprinkle with mushrooms. Place remaining butter in a saucepan and stir in the flour, salt and pepper. Add the cream and cook, stirring constantly, until thickened. Add the cheese and stir until melted. Stir in the Worcestershire sauce and pour over chicken mixture. Bake at 325 degrees for 30 minutes. 4-6 servings.

Mrs. Dorothy Morris, Ooltewah, Tennessee

CHICKEN CASSEROLE DIVINE

2 jars chipped beef	1/2 pt. sour cream
4 chicken breasts	Toasted slivered almonds to
8 strips bacon	taste
1 can cream of mushroom soup	

Cut the chipped beef in small pieces and place in a baking dish. Bone the chicken breasts and cut in half. Wrap each half in bacon slice and place on beef. Combine the soup and sour cream and pour over chicken. Sprinkle with almonds. Bake at 350 degrees for about 1 hour and 30 minutes. 8 servings.

Mrs. L. H. Rainwater, Birmingham, Alabama

SEKANICE

3 lb. veal neck	1 bunch chive tops, finely
2 lb. pork shoulder	chopped
1 loaf bread, crumbled	1/2 onion, grated
2 doz. eggs, well beaten	1/4 tsp. ground nutmeg or
1 clove of garlic, mashed	ginger
1/4 tsp. rubbed marjoram	Dry bread crumbs
Salt and pepper to taste	

Cook the veal and pork in boiling salted water until tender and drain. Bone the veal and pork and chop fine. Soak bread in water and squeeze as dry as possible. Add the veal and pork and remaining ingredients except bread crumbs and mix thoroughly. Line greased baking pans with crumbs and pack veal mixture into pans. Bake in 350-degree oven for 1 hour. 8-10 servings.

Mrs. Herbert Webster, San Antonio, Texas

HOT DISH

1/2 lb. sliced bacon, diced	1 can peas and liquid
1 lb. ground beef	1 can whole kernel corn
1/2 green pepper, chopped	Salt to taste
1 1/4 c. chopped celery	1/2 lb. sharp Cheddar cheese,
2 lge. onions, chopped	grated
2 1/2 c. canned tomatoes	1 c. buttered bread crumbs
1 1/2 c. shell macaroni	

Brown the bacon and ground beef in a skillet. Add chopped vegetables and heat through. Add tomatoes, macaroni, peas, corn and salt and place in a 9 x 13-inch baking dish. Sprinkle with cheese and top with bread crumbs. Bake in 350-degree oven for 1 hour and 30 minutes. 15 servings.

Mrs. Wallace Browder, Houston, Texas

HOT GOODY

1 1/2 lb. hamburger	2 boxes macaroni
1/2 lb. bulk sausage	2 cans cream-style corn
1 onion, diced	2 cans chicken with rice soup
1 lge. green pepper, diced	1 c. bread crumbs
(opt.)	Butter
1 c. diced celery	

Brown the hamburger, sausage and onion in a skillet and add the green pepper and celery. Cook the macaroni according to package directions and add to hamburger mixture. Add remaining ingredients except bread crumbs and butter and mix well. Place in a casserole and top with crumbs. Dot with butter. Bake at 350 degrees for 1 hour. 15-20 servings.

Mrs. Bob Lawrence, Springville, Alabama

BAMMI

1 lb. ground beef	2 tbsp. flour
1 lb. ground lean pork	1 1-qt. can tomatoes
Butter	1 c. boiling water
2 boxes macaroni	2 tsp. curry powder
1 c. finely chopped onion	1 bay leaf
1 tsp. thyme	Salt and pepper to taste

Brown the beef and pork lightly in a small amount of butter. Cook the macaroni according to package directions and drain. Combine 1 tablespoon butter, onion, thyme and flour in a saucepan and cook until lightly browned. Add remaining ingredients. Stir in beef, pork and macaroni and place in a casserole. Bake at 350 degrees for 45 minutes. 15 servings.

Mrs. S. Y. Stribling, Clarkesville, Georgia

LASAGNA CASSEROLE

2 tbsp. olive oil	1/4 tsp. oregano
1/2 lb. ground beef, crumbled	2 c. water
1/2 lb. bulk sausage, crumbled	1 tsp. salt
1 med. onion, chopped	14 wide lasagna strips
1 clove of garlic, minced	1 lb. sliced mozzarella cheese
1 tbsp. chopped parsley	3/4 lb. ricotta cheese
1 1/4 c. tomato paste	4 tbsp. grated Parmesan cheese

Heat the oil in a skillet. Add beef, sausage, onion, garlic and parsley and cook, stirring, until browned. Add the tomato paste, oregano, water and salt and cover. Simmer for 1 hour and 30 minutes. Cook lasagna according to package directions and drain. Place alternate layers of lasagna, beef sauce, mozzarella cheese and ricotta cheese in a well-oiled 3-quart baking pan and sprinkle with Parmesan cheese. Bake at 375 degrees for 20 to 25 minutes or until browned. 4-6 servings.

Mrs. J. V. Blankmeyer, Tampa, Florida

BACON AND BEEF DINNER

1/2 lb. sliced bacon, diced	Flour
2 lb. ground beef	1 can peas
1 tsp. chili powder	1 can tomatoes
1 tsp. salt	1 6-oz. package noodles
1/2 c. chopped onions	1 can cream of mushroom soup
1 c. chopped celery	1 c. grated cheese
1 green pepper, chopped	1 c. buttered bread crumbs

Brown the bacon in a skillet. Add the ground beef, seasonings, onions, celery and green pepper and mix well. Place in a large casserole and sprinkle with small amount of flour. Add the peas and sprinkle with flour. Add the tomatoes and sprinkle with flour. Cook the noodles according to package directions and place over tomatoes. Top with soup and sprinkle with cheese and crumbs. Bake at 350 degrees for 1 hour. 10 servings.

Mrs. Clay Lane, Stanton, Kentucky

BEEF AND PORK CASSEROLE

2 med. onions, chopped	Salt and pepper to taste
4 tbsp. margarine	1 8-oz. package cream cheese
1 lb. ground beef	1 8-oz. package broad egg
1/2 lb. ground lean pork	noodles
2 cans tomato soup	3/4 c. chopped salted almonds
1 tbsp. Worcestershire sauce	1 c. crushed corn flakes
2 tbsp. sugar	3/4 c. mushrooms

Saute the onions in 2 tablespoons margarine in a skillet until golden. Add the beef and pork and cook until brown. Add the soup, Worcestershire sauce, sugar, salt, pepper and cream cheese and mix well. Simmer for 15 minutes or until thickened. Cook the noodles according to package directions and place in a greased casserole. Pour beef mixture over noodles and sprinkle with almonds and corn flake crumbs. Cook the mushrooms in remaining margarine in a saucepan for 2 minutes and place over corn flake crumbs. Bake at 350 degrees for 20 to 25 minutes. 6 servings.

Mrs. Flo I. Hoagland, Jacksonville, Florida

CALIFORNIA CASSEROLE

1 lb. ground beef	1/2 c. margarine
1 lb. ground pork	1 8-oz. package noodles
1 onion, diced	1 15 1/4-oz. can spaghetti
1 c. diced celery	1 lge. can mushrooms, drained
Salt and pepper to taste	3 tbsp. flour
Red pepper to taste	4 c. milk
Minced garlic to taste	1 c. grated sharp cheese

Cook the beef, pork, onion, celery and seasonings in 1/4 cup margarine until meats are brown. Cook the noodles according to package directions and mix with beef mixture. Stir in the spaghetti and mushrooms and pour into 2 large casseroles. Melt remaining margarine in a saucepan and stir in flour. Add the milk and cook, stirring constantly, until thickened. Pour over beef mixture and sprinkle cheese on top. Bake at 350 degrees for 45 minutes. 12-15 servings.

Clara Johnson, Tonkawa, Oklahoma

CHICKEN AND HAM WITH ALMONDS

1 4-lb. chicken	1 tbsp. instant minced onion
Salt and pepper	1/3 tsp. dry mustard
1 stalk celery	3/4 lb. diced cooked ham
1 sm. onion	3/4 lb. sliced mushrooms
Margarine or butter	1/2 c. slivered almonds
1/3 c. flour	1 8-oz. package noodles
1 pt. light cream	

Place the chicken in a kettle and cover with water. Add salt and pepper to taste, celery and onion and bring to a boil. Reduce heat and simmer until chicken is tender. Drain and reserve 1 pint broth. Discard celery and onion. Cool chicken and remove chicken from bones. Melt 1/3 cup margarine in a saucepan and stir in flour. Add the cream and cook, stirring constantly, until thick. Stir in minced onion, mustard, 1 teaspoon salt, 1/4 teaspoon pepper and reserved broth and bring to a boil, stirring constantly. Remove from heat. Add chicken, ham, mushrooms, 3 tablespoons margarine and half the almonds. Cook the noodles according to package directions. Add to chicken mixture and mix well. Pour into a 3-quart casserole and sprinkle with remaining almonds. Bake at 350 degrees for 45 minutes. 8 servings.

Mrs. George Anderson, San Antonio, Texas

SURPRISE CASSEROLE

1 lb. veal steak	1 box fresh mushrooms, chopped
1 lb. lean pork	1/2 green pepper, diced
Salt to taste	1/2 can pimento, diced
1/2 lb. noodles	1/2 lb. sharp cheese, diced
1 can cream of chicken soup	Buttered crumbs
1 can bean sprouts	

Cut the veal and pork in bite-sized pieces and brown in small amount of fat in a skillet. Add salt and place in a large kettle. Cook the noodles according to package directions and add the soup. Drain the bean sprouts and reserve liquid. Add reserved liquid to noodle mixture and mix well. Add to meat mixture and simmer for 30 minutes. Saute the mushrooms until tender and add to meat mixture. Add the bean sprouts, green pepper, pimento and cheese and place in a greased large casserole. Cover with buttered crumbs. Bake at 350 degrees for about 45 minutes. 8 servings.

Mrs. C. A. LaBarre, Portsmouth, Virginia

MOSETTE

2 pkg. noodles	6 onions, sliced
1 can tomato soup	2 green peppers, chopped
1 can tomatoes	2 1/2 lb. ground pork
1 bunch celery, chopped	1 1/2 lb. ground beef
Garlic and salt to taste	Bacon fat
Pinch of soda	1 lb. cheese, grated

Cook the noodles according to package directions. Mix the soup, tomatoes, celery, seasonings and soda in a saucepan and simmer until celery is tender. Brown the onions, green peppers and meats in small amount of fat in a skillet. Mix in the noodles and tomato mixture and pour into a greased baking dish. Bake at 375 degrees until bubbly. Top with grated cheese and bake for 15 minutes longer. 20 servings.

Mrs. H. G. Struble, McAlesta, Oklahoma

FIVE-LAYER CASSEROLE

1 1/2 c. rice	1/2 c. milk
1 lb. ground pork	2 No. 2 1/2 cans sauerkraut
1 1/2 lb. ground beef	1/2 green pepper, chopped fine
1 onion, chopped fine	1 pt. sour cream
Bacon drippings	1 pt. cottage cheese
Salt and pepper to taste	Chopped parsley to taste
1 egg, beaten	Paprika to taste

Cook the rice according to package directions. Saute pork, beef and onion in small amount of bacon drippings in a skillet for 5 minutes and add salt and pepper. Mix the egg and milk and pour into meat mixture. Cook for 5 minutes. Drain the sauerkraut and squeeze dry. Rinse in cold water, drain well and squeeze dry again. Saute in small amount of bacon drippings with green pepper until lightly browned. Place alternate layers of rice, meat mixture, sauerkraut mixture, sour cream and cottage cheese in greased 9 x 13 x 2-inch casserole, sprinkling each layer with parsley, paprika, salt and pepper. Bake in 350-degree oven for 30 minutes. 8-10 servings.

Mrs. Bertha Causey, New Orleans, Louisiana

CALIFORNIA OLIVE PAELLA

1 3-lb. fryer, disjointed	1/8 tsp. white pepper
1/4 c. cooking oil	1 tbsp. chopped parsley
1 c. long grain rice	1 bay leaf
1 lge. onion, chopped	1/8 tsp. saffron (opt.)
1 stalk celery, chopped	1 c. canned pitted ripe olives
2 cloves of garlic, minced	1 4 1/2-oz. can shrimp,
1 1/4 c. hot water	deveined
1 chicken bouillon cube	6 littleneck clams in shells
1/2 c. white table wine	1 c. frozen peas
2 tsp. salt	

Brown the chicken in oil in a skillet over low heat and remove from skillet. Add the rice to skillet and cook, stirring constantly, until browned. Add the onion, celery and garlic and cook until vegetables are wilted. Add the hot water, bouillon cube, wine, salt, pepper, parsley, bay leaf and saffron and bring to a boil. Mix in olives and shrimp and turn into a 2 1/2-quart baking dish. Top with chicken and clams and cover. Bake at 350 degrees for 35 minutes. Stir in peas and cover. Bake for 5 minutes longer. One 10-ounce can whole clams may be used instead of clams in shells, substituting clam liquor for part of the hot water. 4-6 servings.

California Olive Paella (above)

DIRTY RICE

1/2 lb. ground beef	2 cloves of garlic, minced
1 lb. chicken livers, chopped	1 1/2 tsp. salt
1 lb. small frozen shrimp, cleaned	1 tsp. pepper
	1/2 c. salad oil
1 sm. green pepper, chopped	2 c. rice
2 sm. onions, chopped	1 can beef bouillon
2 stalks celery, chopped	

Cook the beef, livers, shrimp, green pepper, onions, celery, garlic, salt and pepper in salad oil in a skillet until tender, but not brown. Cook the rice according to package directions and stir into beef mixture. Sitr in bouillon and simmer for 10 minutes. Place in a casserole. Bake at 350 degrees for 15 to 20 minutes. 6 servings.

Mrs. A. D. Taylor, Pearl River, Louisiana

CHICKEN AND SHRIMP CURRY

1 can cream of chicken soup	1 5-oz. package precooked rice
1/4 c. milk	
1 to 2 tsp. curry powder	1 tbsp. butter
1 6-oz. can boned chicken	1/4 tsp. salt
1 5-oz. can shrimp, drained	2 tbsp. chopped parsley

Blend the soup with milk in a saucepan. Add curry powder, chicken and deveined shrimp and heat through. Cook the rice according to package directions and add butter and salt. Place in a casserole and top with chicken mixture. Bake at 375 degrees for 10 minutes and sprinkle with parsley just before serving. Wild rice may be substituted for rice. 4-6 servings.

Mrs. Nancy W. Darden, Durham, North Carolina

MOCK CHICKEN

1/2 lb. hamburger	2 pkg. chicken-noodle soup mix
1/2 lb. pork sausage	1 c. rice or brown rice
1 lge. onion, chopped	1 c. blanched almonds
1 green pepper, chopped	4 1/2 c. boiling water
2 c. chopped celery	

Brown the meats in a skillet and place in a large casserole. Brown the onion, green pepper and celery in remaining fat in skillet and place over meat mixture. Top with soup mix, rice and almonds and add water. Bake at 325 degrees until rice is tender. 6 servings.

Mrs. Nellie K. Thomas, MacDill AFB, Florida

SAUSAGE PILAF

2 6-oz. packages long grain and wild rice	1 lb. fresh mushrooms, sliced
	6 tbsp. butter
1 lb. sausage links	1/2 tsp. pepper

1 1/2 tsp. salt 1 lb. chicken livers
1 tbsp. instant minced onion

Prepare rice according to package directions and place in a 2-quart casserole. Saute sausages in a skillet until golden brown and place in casserole. Drain skillet and discard fat. Saute mushrooms in same skillet in 1/4 cup butter until golden. Add the pepper, 1/2 teaspoon salt and onion and place on sausages. Saute livers in the skillet in remaining butter until brown on outside but pink inside and sprinkle with remaining salt. Add to rice mixture and toss. Cover. Bake in 325-degree oven for 30 minutes. 6 servings.

Mrs. W. D. Brotherton, Jr., Charleston, South Carolina

ROSY RICE DISH

1/4 lb. sliced bacon 3/4 tsp. salt
1/2 lb. beef liver 1 c. long grain rice
1/4 lb. small sausages 1 No. 303 can tomato juice
1 yellow onion, chopped 3 fresh tomatoes
1/2 tsp. paprika

Cut the bacon and liver in small pieces. Fry the bacon, liver, sausages and onion in a skillet until brown. Sprinkle with paprika and salt and stir in the rice. Add enough water to the tomato juice to make 2 3/4 cups liquid and stir into liver mixture. Pour into a casserole and cover. Bake at 350 degrees for 30 minutes or until rice is tender. Cut the tomatoes in wedges and mix with the rice mixture. 4 servings.

Rosy Rice Dish (above)

SHRIMP WITH PORK AND CHICKEN

2 tbsp. oil	Pinch of saffron
1 clove of garlic, minced	4 c. boiling water
1 sm. green pepper, minced	2 c. rice
1 sm. onion, minced	Salt and pepper to taste
1 c. diced cooked lean pork	1 can green peas, drained
3 cooked chicken breasts,	1 sm. can pimento, minced
diced	20 to 25 cooked med. shrimp

Heat the oil in a large skillet and brown the garlic, green pepper, onion, pork and chicken in oil. Dissolve saffron in boiling water. Add rice to meat mixture and season with salt and pepper. Place in a casserole. Add saffron water and stir well. Add peas, then add pimento. Top with shrimp. Bake in 350-degree oven until rice is done and liquid is absorbed, adding water, if needed. Garnish with paprika and lemon slices. 8 servings.

Mrs. Henry W. Jones, Springfield, Tennessee

TUNA-BACON SOUFFLE

6 slices bacon	1/2 tsp. Worcestershire sauce
2 tbsp. finely chopped onion	1/4 tsp. basil
2 tbsp. finely chopped celery	1/8 tsp. white pepper
1/3 c. butter or margarine	1 7-oz. can tuna
1/3 c. flour	4 eggs, separated
1 c. milk	

Cook the bacon in a skillet until crisp. Drain on paper towels and crumble. Reserve 2 tablespoons bacon drippings. Saute the onion and celery in reserved drippings until crisp-tender. Melt the butter in a medium saucepan and stir in the flour. Add milk gradually and cook over medium heat, stirring constantly, until thickened. Cook for 1 minute, then remove from heat. Stir in the bacon, onion mixture and seasonings. Drain and flake the tuna and stir into bacon mixture. Beat the egg yolks lightly and stir into tuna mixture. Beat the egg whites until stiff but not dry and fold into tuna mixture. Pour into a 1 1/2-quart greased casserole. Bake in 350-degree oven for 45 minutes. 4 servings.

Photograph for this recipe on page 136.

SPAGHETTI WITH HAM AND CHICKEN

1 1/2 c. spaghetti	1 c. cottage cheese
1/4 c. butter	1 1/2 c. chopped cooked ham
6 green onions and tops,	1 1/2 c. chopped cooked chicken
chopped	Salt and pepper to taste
1 sm. can mushrooms	Garlic and celery salt to taste
1 c. sour cream	1 c. shredded cheese

Cook the spaghetti according to package directions. Heat the butter in a large skillet. Add onions and mushrooms and cook until tender. Add sour cream and cottage cheese to spaghetti and mix. Add meats and onion mixture. Add seasonings and toss lightly. Turn into buttered casserole and top with cheese. Bake at 350 degrees until bubbly.

Mrs. Dean Patrick, Heidelberg, Mississippi

CHICKEN AND SEAFOOD TETRAZZINI

1 4-lb. hen	2 lb. cooked cleaned shrimp
1 pkg. spaghetti	1 can crab meat
1 sm. onion, chopped	1 can mushroom soup
1 clove of garlic	1 can tomato soup
Bacon drippings	1 tbsp. Worcestershire sauce
1 can oysters, drained	1 c. grated sharp cheese

Cook the hen in boiling, salted water until tender. Drain and reserve broth. Remove chicken from bones and cut in small pieces. Cook spaghetti in reserved broth until done and drain. Saute onion and garlic in small amount of bacon drippings until tender. Add oysters and cook until oysters curl. Combine chicken and oyster mixture with remaining ingredients except cheese and place in a casserole. Top with cheese. Bake at 350 degrees for 45 minutes or until heated through and serve over spaghetti. 12 servings.

Mrs. Malcolm Sevier, Tallulah, Louisiana

CHICKEN AND HAM WITH BROCCOLI

2 4-lb. hens, cooked	1/2 c. chicken broth
4 10-oz. packages broccoli	Dash of red pepper
1 lb. sliced cooked ham	Salt to taste
1 lb. Velveeta cheese, cubed	Bread crumbs
1 c. milk	

Remove chicken from bones and cut in large pieces. Place alternate layers of chicken, broccoli and ham in a large casserole. Mix remaining ingredients except crumbs in a double boiler and cook until cheese is melted, stirring frequently. Pour over layers in casserole and cover with bread crumbs. Bake at 350 degrees for 1 hour. Asparagus may be substituted for broccoli.

Mrs. Paul A. FitzGerald, Albuquerque, New Mexico

RED GATE FARM SCALLOPED CHICKEN

2 c. chopped cooked chicken	Salt and pepper to taste
1 c. cooked sausage	3 c. sliced cooked potatoes
2 c. chicken gravy	Buttered bread cubes
1 tsp. onion juice	

Combine the meats, gravy and onion juice and season with salt and pepper. Place alternate layers of meat mixture and potatoes in buttered baking dish and cover with bread cubes. Bake at 350 degrees for 30 minutes or until bread is brown.

Mrs. William B. Marks, Harrisonburg, Virginia

MONTEZUMA SPECIAL

1/2 lb. lean ground beef, crumbled	3 tomato sauce cans water
1/2 lb. pork sausage, crumbled	1 doz. corn tortillas
1 pkg. spaghetti sauce mix	1 med. onion, chopped
1/4 tsp. seasoned salt	1 4 1/2-oz. can chopped ripe olives
1 1/2 tbsp. chili powder	2 c. grated Cheddar cheese
1/4 tsp. cumin seed	1/2 c. small whole ripe olives
2 8-oz. cans tomato sauce	

Brown the beef and sausage in a skillet and add spaghetti sauce mix, seasoned salt, chili powder, cumin seed, tomato sauce and water. Mix thoroughly and bring to a boil. Reduce heat and simmer for 20 minutes. Place 1/2 cup meat mixture in a 3-quart casserole and cover sides and bottom of casserole with 6 tortillas. Place half the remaining meat mixture on tortillas and sprinkle with half the onion, half the chopped olives and half the cheese. Repeat layers and top with whole olives. Bake at 350 degrees for 30 to 40 minutes. 6-8 servings.

Mrs. Robert Glass, Pensacola, Florida

CREAMED CHICKEN CASSEROLE

2 lb. chicken breasts	1/4 lb. sliced mushrooms
Salt and pepper to taste	4 tbsp. flour
Butter or margarine	2 c. cream
1 No. 2 can sm. potatoes	1 c. dry white wine
1/2 c. diced cooked ham	1 pkg. frozen sm. green peas

Season the chicken breasts with salt and pepper and brown in 1/4 cup butter in a skillet. Place in a deep casserole. Drain the potatoes and brown in same skillet. Place on chicken. Add the ham, mushrooms, salt and pepper. Melt 3 tablespoons butter in a saucepan and blend in flour. Add cream and wine and cook, stirring constantly, until smooth and thickened. Pour over casserole and cover. Bake in 350-degree oven for 1 hour to 1 hour and 15 minutes or until chicken is tender. Cook the peas according to package directions and place on chicken mixture. Bake for 10 minutes longer.

Mrs. A. G. Detrich, Tyler, Texas

TAMALE JOE CASSEROLE

1/2 lb. link sausage	2 8-oz. cans tomato sauce
1 1/2 lb. ground beef	1 c. milk
1 lge. onion, chopped	1 12-oz. can whole kernel corn
1 bell pepper, chopped	
1 tbsp. chili powder	1/2 c. cornmeal
2 tsp. salt	1/2 c. chopped olives
1/4 tsp. pepper	1 c. grated cheese

Brown the sausage in a skillet and drain off fat. Add the beef, onion and bell pepper and cook and stir until beef is partially done. Add seasonings, tomato sauce and milk. Drain the corn and stir into beef mixture. Simmer for 20 minutes. Stir in cornmeal and add olives. Pour into a casserole and top with cheese. Bake in 325-degree oven for 40 minutes.

Mrs. Steve Bandin, Bordelonville, Louisiana

GIRALDA RICE WITH CHICKEN AND SAUSAGE

1 lb. chorizo or garlic- flavored sausage, sliced	1/4 c. chopped parsley
1 med. eggplant	1/4 tsp. thyme leaves
1 tsp. salt	1/8 tsp. pepper
1/2 c. olive oil	3 c. chicken bouillon
2 lge. peeled tomatoes, chopped	3 c. diced cooked chicken
	1/2 c. sliced stuffed olives
1 med. onion, chopped	2 lge. tomatoes, sliced
1 1/2 c. rice	1/2 c. whole stuffed olives
2 med. green peppers, chopped	3 oz. Gruyere cheese, grated

Brown the chorizo in a large skillet. Remove from skillet and drain on paper towels. Drain fat from skillet. Cut the eggplant in 1/2-inch slices and sprinkle with salt. Fry in 1/3 cup oil in the skillet and remove from skillet. Drain. Combine remaining oil, chopped tomatoes, onion and rice in same skillet and saute for 2 minutes. Mix in the sausage, green peppers, parsley, thyme, pepper and bouillon and cover. Simmer for 20 minutes or until rice is tender, stirring occasionally. Stir in the chicken and sliced olives and turn into 3 1/2-quart baking dish. Overlap eggplant and tomato slices around edges of dish and place whole olives in center. Sprinkle cheese on top. Bake at 350 degrees for 5 to 10 minutes or until cheese is melted.

Giralda Rice with Chicken and Sausage (above)

vegetables

Hearty vegetable casseroles add so much to a meal! And southern homemakers who take pride in their home-grown vegetables have developed a rich assortment of casserole recipes especially for family meals. Reading through these recipes, which have been brought together in the following section, is sure to be mouth-watering.

Are you and your family squash lovers? Then you will be certain to enjoy Baked Tomatoes and Zucchini, a spicy dish reminiscent of Italian cuisine. Another favorite of southern families is the sweet potato — no special occasion is really complete without it. Next time you serve sweet potatoes, try flavorful Apple and Sweet Potato Pone.

The wide variety of bean casserole recipes, with all the different kinds of beans available, will give you many ideas for new ways to serve these all-time favorites. You might try Dill Bean Casserole, a sharply flavored dish featuring the flavors of Creole-style cooking.

As you browse through these pages, you will be excited to discover the wonderful variety of recipes awaiting you. Recipes for cucumbers ... cabbage ... eggplant ... peas ... beans ... all your favorite vegetables and perhaps some new ones you haven't tried before. Your family will be certain to come back for seconds and thirds when you feature vegetables in these casseroles!

151

Artichokes and Chicken for the Seventies (below)

ARTICHOKES AND CHICKEN FOR THE SEVENTIES

6 med. artichokes	1/4 lb. fresh mushrooms, sliced
4 1/2 to 5 lb. frying chicken pieces	1 1/2 tsp. salt
	1/4 tsp. pepper
1/4 lb. butter or margarine	1/4 tsp. crushed thyme leaves
4 carrots, cut in strips	2 chicken bouillon cubes
1 9 1/2-oz. can water chestnuts (opt.)	1 c. dry white wine (opt.)
	2 tbsp. cornstarch
1 bunch scallions, sliced	

Remove 2 or 3 layers of outer artichoke leaves and cut off stem and top half of each artichoke. Cut in quarters and cook in 2 to 3 inches of boiling, salted water for 15 to 20 minutes or until tender. Drain and remove chokes. Brown the chicken in 4 tablespoons butter in a large skillet. Cover the skillet and cook chicken over low heat for about 10 minutes. Remove chicken from skillet and set aside. Add remaining butter and carrots to the skillet and cover. Cook for 5 minutes. Drain and slice the water chestnuts and add to carrots. Add the scallions, mushrooms and seasonings and saute for 1 minute. Remove vegetables with a slotted spoon and set aside. Dissolve the bouillon cubes in 1 cup boiling water and pour into the skillet. Stir 2 cups cold water and the wine into cornstarch and add to bouillon. Mix well. Cook, stirring occasionally, until clear and thickened. Arrange the artichokes, chicken and sauteed vegetables in a large casserole and pour bouillon mixture over all. Cover tightly. Bake in 375-degree oven for 1 hour or until chicken is tender, basting occasionally. 6 servings.

ARTICHOKE HEARTS AND PECANS

2 No. 2 cans artichoke hearts, drained	1 c. cream
	2 tbsp. butter

2 tbsp. flour
Salt and pepper to taste
Hot sauce to taste

1/2 c. broken pecans
1/4 c. bread crumbs
2 tbsp. Parmesan cheese

Stand artichoke hearts in small casserole. Blend the cream, butter and flour in a saucepan and cook until thickened, stirring constantly. Season with salt, pepper and hot sauce and pour over artichoke hearts. Add pecans and sprinkle with bread crumbs and cheese. Bake at 300 degrees until bubbly. 6 servings.

Selma Sailors, Diller, Nebraska

ARTICHOKE CASSEROLE SUPREME

12 artichokes
1 tsp. salt
1 c. boiling water
1 clove of garlic, crushed
1 tbsp. salad oil

1/4 c. lemon juice
Chopped cooked seafood,
    chicken or turkey
Medium white sauce

Cut stems of artichokes to 1/2 inch and remove outer leaves and thorny leaf tips. Tie artichokes with string to keep leaves in place. Place in a saucepan and add salt, boiling water, garlic, oil and lemon juice. Cover and cook for 30 minutes. Remove artichokes from water and remove string. Place alternate layers of artichoke hearts, seafood and sauce in a baking dish. Bake at 350 degrees for 20 minutes. 6 servings.

Mrs. Kelley Storey, Paris, Texas

ASPARAGUS CASSEROLE

1 No. 2 can green asparagus
    tips
4 hard-boiled eggs, sliced

3/4 lb. American cheese, grated
1 can cream of mushroom soup

Drain the asparagus. Place alternate layers of asparagus, eggs and cheese in casserole and cover with soup. Bake at 350 degrees until cheese is melted. 6-8 servings.

Mrs. Eddie Hadwin, Estill, South Carolina

FRIED ONION-ASPARAGUS CASSEROLE

2 sm. cans asparagus tips
1 1/2 c. grated American cheese
1 can mushroom soup

1 sm. can evaporated milk
1 3 1/2-oz. can French-fried
    onion rings

Drain the asparagus and place in a well-greased casserole. Cover with cheese. Mix the soup and milk and pour over cheese. Bake at 350 degrees for 30 minutes. Sprinkle onion rings over top and bake for 10 minutes longer. 8-10 servings.

Mrs. S. L. Norrell, Cleburne, Texas

EGG AND ASPARAGUS CASSEROLE

1 c. bread crumbs	3 tbsp. flour
3/4 c. melted butter	1 1/2 c. milk
2 cans cut asparagus	1 glass sharp process cheese
3 hard-boiled eggs, sliced	Dash of oregano
1 pkg. slivered almonds (opt.)	Dash of cayenne pepper

Combine the crumbs and 1/2 cup butter and line a casserole with half the crumbs. Cover with asparagus and add eggs and almonds. Blend flour into remaining butter in a saucepan. Stir in the milk and cook, stirring constantly, until thickened. Add cheese and cook until cheese is melted. Pour over asparagus and top with remaining crumbs. Sprinkle with oregano and cayenne pepper. Bake at 450 degrees for 12 minutes.

Mrs. Clyde Wildharber, Barlow, Kentucky

SWISS ASPARAGUS CASSEROLE

4 tbsp. butter or margarine	2 tbsp. chopped celery
1/2 tsp. salt	1 tbsp. chopped pimento (opt.)
1/4 tsp. paprika	2 hard-cooked eggs, chopped
3 tbsp. flour	1 tbsp. chopped onion
1 1/2 c. milk	1 lge. can asparagus
1 can mushroom soup	1 c. buttered crumbs
1/2 lb. Swiss cheese, cubed	

Melt the butter in a saucepan and stir in salt, paprika and flour. Add the milk and cook, stirring constantly, until smooth and thick. Add soup and cheese and stir until cheese is melted. Add the celery, pimento, eggs and onion. Place alternate layers of sauce and asparagus in casserole and top with buttered crumbs. Bake at 400 degrees for 20 to 30 minutes.

Mrs. James L. Norman, Calhoun City, Mississippi

EGGS AND ASPARAGUS AU GRATIN

1 No. 2 can asparagus	Milk
2 tbsp. butter or margarine	1 c. grated cheese
2 tbsp. all-purpose flour	4 hard-cooked eggs, sliced
1/2 tsp. salt	1/2 c. soft bread crumbs
Dash of pepper	

Preheat oven to 350 degrees. Drain the asparagus and reserve liquid. Melt the butter in a saucepan and blend in flour, salt and pepper. Mix reserved liquid with enough milk to make 1 1/2 cups liquid and add to flour mixture. Cook, stirring constantly, until thickened. Remove from heat and add cheese. Place alternate layers of eggs, asparagus and cheese sauce in a greased baking dish and cover with crumbs. Bake for 25 minutes. 6 servings.

Mrs. Ruby B. Epting, Chapin, South Carolina

SCALLOPED TOMATOES

1 c. diced celery	3 1/2 c. tomatoes
1/2 c. finely chopped onion	1 tbsp. sugar
2 tbsp. butter	1 tsp. salt
2 tbsp. flour	1/8 tsp. pepper
3 slices buttered toast	

Cook the celery and onion in butter in a saucepan until just tender and blend in flour. Cut toast into cubes. Mix the tomatoes, half the toast cubes, sugar, seasonings and onion mixture and place in a 1 1/2-quart casserole. Bake at 350 degrees for 30 minutes. Top with remaining toast cubes and bake for 20 minutes longer. 8 servings.

Gracie Metheney, Rupert, West Virginia

CREOLE LIMA-BEEF CASSEROLE

1 1/2 lb. ground beef	2 med. onions, chopped
1 1/4 tsp. hot sauce	1 clove of garlic, peeled
2 1/2 tsp. salt	1 1-lb. can seasoned
1/4 tsp. dry mustard	stewed tomatoes
1/2 tsp. leaf thyme	1 6-oz. can tomato paste
1 tbsp. minced parsley	1 10-oz. package frozen
2 tbsp. butter or margarine	lima beans, thawed

Mix the ground beef with 3/4 teaspoon hot sauce, 1 1/2 teaspoons salt, mustard, thyme and parsley. Saute the ground beef mixture in the butter in a skillet with onions and garlic until beef is browned and remove the garlic. Place half the beef mixture in a 1 1/2-quart casserole. Combine the tomatoes, tomato paste and remaining hot sauce and salt and pour over beef mixture. Sprinkle with lima beans. Place remaining beef mixture in center and cover. Bake at 350 degrees for 45 minutes. 6 servings.

Creole Lima-Beef Casserole (above)

BEAN CASSEROLE

1 can pork and beans	Salt to taste
1 can red kidney beans	1/2 tsp. garlic salt
1 pkg. frozen lima beans	1 1/2 c. brown sugar
1 1/2 c. chopped green peppers	1 c. catsup
1 1/2 c. chopped celery	Bacon strips
1 1/2 c. chopped onions	

Drain the pork and beans and kidney beans. Cook the lima beans according to package directions and drain. Mix all ingredients except bacon and place in a large baking dish. Cover with bacon. Bake at 350 degrees for 45 minutes. 12 servings.

Mrs. Elizabeth W. Mobley, McKinney, Kentucky

DILL GREEN BEANS

2 cans sliced green beans	3 tbsp. grated onion
1 tsp. dillseed	2 tsp. monosodium glutamate
1 tbsp. bacon grease	Salt and pepper to taste
6 tbsp. margarine	Dash of hot sauce
6 tbsp. flour	1 c. buttered bread crumbs
1 c. milk	

Place the beans, dillseed and bacon grease in a saucepan and cook until liquid is reduced to 1 cup. Drain and reserve liquid. Place the beans in casserole. Melt the margarine in the saucepan and blend in flour. Stir in reserved bean liquid and milk. Add the onion, monosodium glutamate, salt, pepper and hot sauce and cook until thick. Pour over beans and cover with crumbs. Bake at 350 degrees for 20 to 25 minutes. 6-8 servings.

Mrs. Ernest Highers, Ozark, Arkansas

BROCCOLI-DEVILED EGG CASSEROLE

6 hard-cooked eggs	2 tbsp. flour
3 tbsp. mayonnaise	2 c. milk
1/8 tsp. dry mustard	1 c. grated sharp cheese
Dash of pepper	1/2 tsp. Worcestershire sauce
2 10-oz. packages chopped broccoli	1/2 tsp. salt
1/4 c. butter	Dash of hot sauce

Cut eggs in half lengthwise, remove yolks and mash well. Add mayonnaise, mustard and pepper and blend well. Fill egg whites with yolk mixture. Cook broccoli according to package directions and drain well. Melt the butter in a saucepan. Add the flour and stir until blended. Add milk gradually and cook over medium heat until thickened, stirring constantly. Reserve 2 tablespoons cheese. Add remaining cheese to sauce and stir until cheese is melted. Add Worcestershire sauce, salt and hot sauce. Place broccoli in a well-greased 1 1/2-quart baking dish and add half the cheese sauce. Arrange eggs on sauce and pour remaining sauce over eggs. Sprinkle with reserved cheese. Bake at 375 degrees for 20 to 25 minutes or until lightly browned. 6 servings.

Mrs. J. C. West, Ferguson, North Carolina

CHEESED BROCCOLI

2 pkg. frozen chopped broccoli	1 tsp. monosodium glutamate
2 beaten eggs	1 tsp. Worcestershire sauce
1 c. mayonnaise or salad dressing	1 tbsp. minced onion
1/2 c. milk	Salt and pepper to taste
1 c. grated sharp Cheddar cheese	1 stack round buttery crackers, crumbled
1 c. celery soup	Butter

Cook the broccoli according to package directions and drain. Combine remaining ingredients except cracker crumbs and butter and mix with broccoli. Place in a greased casserole and sprinkle with crumbs. Dot with butter. Bake at 350 degrees for 45 to 50 minutes. 10-12 servings.

Mary Ward Smith, Clarksville, Tennessee

BROCCOLI CASSEROLE

1 pkg. frozen broccoli	1/2 tsp. salt
1 1/4 c. milk	1/2 tsp. grated nutmeg
3 eggs, lightly beaten	1/2 c. grated cheese

Preheat oven to 350 degrees. Cook the broccoli in boiling water for 3 minutes and drain. Pour the milk into a saucepan and bring to a boil. Cool to lukewarm. Mix the eggs with the salt and nutmeg. Add the milk and cheese, beating constantly, and pour into a greased baking dish. Add the broccoli. Bake for about 30 minutes or until a knife inserted in center comes out clean. 4 servings.

Broccoli Casserole (above)

BRUSSELS SPROUTS CASSEROLE

3 boxes frozen Brussels sprouts	1/2 roll sharp cheese, grated
1/4 c. lemon juice	Dash of dry mustard
Salt and pepper to taste	1/2 tsp. Worcestershire sauce
1/4 c. butter	Dash of hot sauce
2 tbsp. flour	Buttered bread crumbs
1 c. evaporated milk	Paprika
1/2 sm. package Velveeta, grated	

Cook the Brussels sprouts according to package directions and place in a casserole. Sprinkle with lemon juice, salt and pepper. Melt the butter in a saucepan and stir in the flour. Add the milk and cook, stirring constantly, until thickened. Add salt, pepper, cheeses, mustard, Worcestershire sauce and hot sauce and stir until cheeses are melted. Pour over Brussels sprouts and cover with buttered crumbs. Sprinkle with paprika. Bake at 350 degrees until bubbly. 8 servings.

Mrs. Frank Parrot, Salisbury, North Carolina

CABBAGE-APPLE CASSEROLE

1 sm. red cabbage	Juice of 1 lemon
1 sm. green cabbage	Nutmeg to taste
Salt and pepper to taste	3 c. diced apples
1/2 c. butter	1 c. minced green pepper
1/2 c. brown sugar	1 c. buttered bread crumbs

Grind red and green cabbage separately. Season the red cabbage with salt and pepper and place in a greased casserole. Dot with half the butter. Add the brown sugar, lemon juice and nutmeg to apples and mix well. Place on red cabbage. Mix the green cabbage, green pepper, salt and pepper and place over apples. Dot with remaining butter and cover with bread crumbs. Bake in 375-degree oven for 25 minutes. 4-6 servings.

Mrs. Ray Gragg, Bell City, Louisiana

CABBAGE CASSEROLE

1 med. cabbage, shredded	1 1/2 c. grated American cheese
1 c. chopped celery	1 1/2 c. evaporated milk
2 green peppers, chopped	Dash of Worcestershire sauce
2 med. onions, chopped	Salt and pepper to taste
Chopped garlic to taste	1 c. bread crumbs

Cook the cabbage in small amount of water in a saucepan until tender and drain. Saute the celery, green peppers, onions and garlic in small amount of fat in a saucepan until tender and mix with cabbage. Pour into a casserole. Combine the cheese, milk, Worcestershire sauce, salt and pepper and pour over cabbage mixture. Cover with crumbs. Bake at 350 degrees for 30 minutes. 8 servings.

Mrs. C. B. Owens, Leesville, Louisiana

CRUSTY SWEET POTATO CASSEROLE

6 med. cooked sweet potatoes	2 tbsp. melted butter
1 tsp. salt	1 tbsp. orange juice
1/4 tsp. mace	1/3 c. finely chopped peanuts
1 egg, slightly beaten	1/3 c. flaked coconut
1/3 c. crushed pineapple	2 tbsp. brown sugar
1/8 tsp. ginger	

Mash the sweet potatoes and blend in the salt, mace, egg, pineapple, ginger, butter and orange juice. Place in a greased 1 1/2-quart casserole. Bake at 400 degrees for 20 to 30 minutes. Combine the peanuts, coconut and brown sugar and sprinkle over casserole. Bake for 8 to 10 minutes longer or until lightly browned. 6 servings.

Mrs. E. E. McHenry, Cumberland, Virginia

SWEET-SOUR YAMS AND PINEAPPLE

1 20-oz. can sliced pineapple	4 green onions, diagonally sliced
1 tbsp. cornstarch	1/2 c. diagonally sliced celery
1/4 tsp. salt	
3 tbsp. vinegar	1/2 c. green pepper chunks
2 16-oz. cans yams, drained	1 tbsp. oil

Drain the pineapple and reserve syrup. Combine reserved syrup with cornstarch and salt in a saucepan and cook, stirring, until sauce boils and thickens. Stir in the vinegar. Add the yams and pineapple slices and pour into a casserole. Cover. Bake at 350 degrees for about 25 minutes. Cook the onions, celery and green pepper in oil in a saucepan for about 4 minutes. Stir into yam mixture and serve at once. 8 servings.

Sweet-Sour Yams and Pineapple (above)

APPLE AND SWEET POTATO CASSEROLE

1 2-lb. can sweet potatoes	**1/4 c. melted butter**
2 c. sliced peeled apples	**1 tsp. salt**
3/4 c. maple-blended syrup	

Drain the sweet potatoes and slice lengthwise. Place in a greased 12 x 8 x 2-inch baking dish. Place apple slices on potatoes. Combine the syrup, butter and salt and pour over apples. Cover. Bake in 350-degree oven for 45 minutes. Remove cover and bake for about 30 minutes longer or until apples are tender, basting frequently and adding syrup, if needed. 8 servings.

Mrs. A. P. Moore, Sparks, Oklahoma

FRESH CORN CASSEROLE

12 sm. onions	**1 bay leaf**
1 c. sliced carrots	**Juice of 1 lemon**
1 c. sliced celery	**2 cans beef bouillon**
1 c. cut green beans	**1 c. sliced cooked chicken**
1 green pepper, cut in chunks	**1 c. cubed cooked beef**
Salt and pepper to taste	**3 ears corn, cut in half**

Place the onions, carrots, celery, green beans and green pepper in a casserole. Add the salt, pepper, bay leaf and lemon juice and mix well. Pour in the beef bouillon and add enough water to cover. Cover the casserole. Bake at 350 degrees for about 1 hour or until vegetables are tender. Uncover and add the chicken and beef. Stir well. Place the corn on top and cover. Bake for 20 minutes longer or until corn is tender. 6 servings.

Fresh Corn Casserole (above)

BAKED CORN EN CASSEROLE

1 No. 303 can cream-style corn	1 egg, well beaten
1 No. 303 can whole kernel corn	1 c. cracker crumbs
1 lge. onion, chopped	1 c. grated cheese
1 med. bell pepper, chopped	1/4 c. melted margarine or butter
1 2-oz. jar pimento, chopped	2 tbsp. sugar
2/3 c. milk	Salt and pepper to taste
	Red pepper to taste

Combine all ingredients and mix well. Place in a greased 2-quart casserole. Bake at 350 degrees for 1 hour. 8 servings.

Mrs. Joe P. Hollingsworth, Bryan, Texas

FRESH CORN-CHEESE QUICHE

4 ears fresh corn	2 tbsp. chopped pimento
5 eggs, beaten	1 tsp. salt
1 1/2 c. half and half	1/8 tsp. ground pepper
1/4 c. grated Parmesan cheese	1 9-in. unbaked pie shell
2 tbsp. finely chopped onion	6 strips crisp bacon

Preheat oven to 400 degrees. Cut the corn kernels off cobs and set aside. Mix the eggs with half and half in a bowl. Add the cheese, onion, pimento, salt and pepper and mix well. Stir in the corn kernels and pour into pie shell. Bake for 25 minutes. Reduce temperature to 350 degrees. Arrange bacon over corn mixture and bake for 20 minutes longer or until a knife inserted in center comes out clean. 6 servings.

Photograph for this recipe on page 150.

BAKED HOMINY AND CHEESE CASSEROLE

3 tbsp. butter	1 tsp. Worcestershire sauce
6 tbsp. flour	1/2 tsp. grated onion
1 tsp. salt	1/2 lb. grated American cheese
1/8 tsp. pepper	2 No. 2 cans hominy, drained
1/2 tsp. dry mustard	1/3 c. dry bread crumbs
2 c. milk	

Melt the butter in a saucepan and blend in flour, salt, pepper and mustard. Add the milk gradually and cook over low heat until thick, stirring constantly. Stir in Worcestershire sauce, onion and cheese. Place the hominy in a greased 1 1/2-quart casserole and pour cheese sauce over hominy. Sprinkle crumbs on top. Bake in a 350-degree oven for 30 minutes. 6 servings.

Minnie E. Hancock, Winston-Salem, North Carolina

BAKED APPLE AND CARROT CASSEROLE

5 apples, thinly sliced	2 tbsp. flour
2 c. sliced cooked carrots	Salt to taste
6 tbsp. sugar	3/4 c. orange juice

Place half the apple slices in a baking dish and cover with half the carrots. Mix the sugar, flour and salt and sprinkle half the mixture over the carrots. Repeat layers and pour the orange juice over top. Bake at 350 degrees for 20 to 30 minutes. 5 servings.

Mrs. Junnie M. Goldston, Leaksville, North Carolina

BUFFET SCALLOPED CARROTS

12 med. carrots, sliced	2 c. milk
1/4 c. butter or margarine	1/8 tsp. pepper
1 sm. onion, minced	1/4 tsp. celery salt
1/4 c. flour	1 1/2-lb. package American
1 tsp. salt	process cheese slices
1/4 tsp. dry mustard	3 c. buttered bread crumbs

Preheat oven to 350 degrees. Place the carrots in a saucepan and cover with water. Bring to a boil and cover. Reduce heat and simmer for 20 minutes. Drain. Melt the butter in a saucepan. Add the onion and cook over low heat for 2 to 3 minutes. Stir in flour, salt and mustard. Add the milk and cook, stirring, until smooth. Add the pepper and celery salt. Place 1/3 of the carrots in a 2-quart casserole and add 1/2 of the cheese. Repeat layers, ending with carrots. Pour sauce over carrots and top with crumbs. Bake for about 25 minutes or until crumbs are golden brown. 6-8 servings.

Mrs. George L. Shank, Williamsport, Maryland

CARROT AND CHEESE CASSEROLE

8 carrots	1 c. medium white sauce
American cheese slices	1/2 tsp. prepared mustard

Scrape the carrots and slice crosswise. Cook in a small amount of boiling, salted water until just tender and drain. Place layers of carrots and cheese in a greased baking dish, beginning and ending with carrots. Mix the white sauce and prepared mustard and pour over carrots. Bake at 300 degrees for 30 minutes.

Mrs. John F. Baker, Umbarger, Texas

CAULIFLOWER CASSEROLE

1 med. cauliflower	1/2 c. grated sharp cheese
1 can frozen cream of	Butter or margarine
shrimp soup	

Separate the cauliflower into flowerets and cook in boiling, salted water until just tender. Place in a shallow baking dish. Thaw the soup and pour over cauli-flowerets. Sprinkle with cheese and dot with butter. Bake in 350-degree oven for about 30 minutes or until bubbly. 6 servings.

Mrs. Ralph McCoy, Sr., Elkton, Virginia

CAULIFLOWER AND HAM CASSEROLE

1 lge. cauliflower	1/2 c. buttered bread crumbs
1 c. chopped cooked ham	1/2 c. grated Cheddar cheese
1 can cream of mushroom soup	

Cook the cauliflower in boiling water for about 20 minutes and drain. Separate into flowerets. Place alternate layers of cauliflowerets and ham in a casserole and cover with soup. Sprinkle with bread crumbs and cheese. Bake in a 375-degree oven for 25 minutes or until lightly browned. 4-6 servings.

Mrs. William Segal, Jacksonville, Florida

SCALLOPED EGGPLANT

1 eggplant	1 egg, beaten
1/2 c. chopped onion	2 1/2 tsp. salt
2 tbsp. chopped green pepper	1/2 tsp. crumbled oregano leaves
1/2 lb. ground lean chuck	1/2 tsp. pepper
1 tbsp. olive or salad oil	1/4 c. grated American cheese
1 1/2 c. cut fresh corn	

Preheat oven to 350 degrees. Cut the eggplant in 1-inch cubes and cook in boiling salted water until tender. Drain. Saute the onion, green pepper and ground chuck in oil in a skillet until chuck is partially cooked. Add the corn and cook, stirring, for 5 minutes. Add the eggplant, egg, salt, oregano and pepper and mix well. Add the cheese and spoon into a baking dish. Bake for 30 minutes or until lightly browned. Garnish with tomato wedges. 6 servings.

Photograph for this recipe on page 5.

EXCELLENT EGGPLANT CASSEROLE

1 med. eggplant	1 6-oz. package sliced
1 egg, beaten	mozzarella cheese
1/2 c. fine dry bread crumbs	1 env. spaghetti sauce mix
1/3 c. oil	1 1/2 c. water

Peel the eggplant and cut into 1/2-inch thick slices. Dip each slice into egg, then into crumbs and brown on both sides in oil in a skillet. Place half the eggplant in a 2-quart casserole and top with half the cheese. Add remaining eggplant. Mix the spaghetti sauce mix with water in a saucepan and bring to a boil. Pour over eggplant. Arrange remaining cheese slices over the top and cover casserole. Bake in a 350-degree oven for 20 minutes. 4-5 servings.

Mrs. A. Frank Arnold, Spruce Pine, North Carolina

CORN AND ZUCCHINI CASSEROLE

4 tbsp. butter	1/2 tsp. salt
1/4 c. thinly sliced green onions	Dash of pepper
1 1/2 c. sliced zucchini	1 tbsp. finely chopped parsley
3 c. cut fresh corn	1 c. buttered bread crumbs
1 med. tomato, chopped	

Melt the butter in a heavy skillet and saute the onions in butter until soft. Add the zucchini and cook until just tender. Mix the corn, tomato, salt, pepper and parsley. Place alternate layers of zucchini mixture and corn mixture in a casserole and top with buttered bread crumbs. Bake at 350 degrees until corn is done. 6 servings.

Mrs. J. W. Triplett, Signal Mountain, Tennessee

FIESTA CASSEROLE

1 No. 2 can tomatoes	4 eggs
1 No. 2 can cream-style corn	1 green pepper, chopped
2 jars Cheddar cheese spread	2 pimentos, chopped
2 c. cooked rice	2 tbsp. chopped onion
	4 tbsp. melted margarine
	Salt and pepper to taste

Combine all ingredients and mix well. Pour into a greased casserole. Bake at 325 degrees for 1 hour.

Mrs. Valerin W. Hamiter, Reform, Alabama

GREEN AND YELLOW CASSEROLE

2 boxes frozen chopped broccoli	Dash of salt
2 cans yellow cream-style corn	Dash of garlic salt
2 c. shredded mild Cheddar cheese	Dash of thyme
	Dash of nutmeg
	3 eggs, beaten
	Buttered bread crumbs

Place 1 package broccoli in a greased shallow casserole and add 1 can corn. Sprinkle 1 cup cheese over corn and add seasonings. Add remaining broccoli, then add remaining corn. Sprinkle remaining cheese on corn and pour eggs over cheese. Cover with buttered bread crumbs. Bake at 350 degrees for 30 minutes. Cover and bake for 15 minutes longer. 12 servings.

Mrs. Marvin L. Sharp, Vernon, Texas

SPRING CASSEROLE

1 sm. cauliflower	8 sm. carrots
8 sm. new potatoes	8 sm. onions

1 c. fresh or frozen peas	2 c. milk
4 tbsp. butter	1/2 lb. American cheese,
4 tbsp. flour	grated
1 tsp. salt	Parsley

Separate the cauliflower into flowerets and place in a saucepan. Add the potatoes, carrots, onions and peas and cover with water. Bring to a boil and reduce heat. Simmer until tender and drain well. Place in a casserole. Melt the butter in a saucepan and stir in the flour and salt. Stir in milk gradually and cook, stirring constantly, until thick and smooth. Add the cheese and stir until cheese is melted. Pour over vegetables. Bake in 350-degree oven for 20 minutes or until heated through and garnish with parsley.

Evelyn J. Bailey, Louisville, Kentucky

SAVORY CREAMED MUSHROOMS

1/4 c. butter	2 c. grated American process
1 tbsp. chopped onion	cheese
1/4 c. chopped green pepper	3 hard-cooked eggs, sliced
1/4 c. flour	3 tbsp. finely diced pimento
2 c. milk	1/4 c. sliced stuffed olives
2 4-oz. cans mushrooms,	2 5-oz. cans chow mein
drained	noodles

Melt the butter in a saucepan over low heat. Add the onion and green pepper and cook until tender but not brown. Blend in flour. Add the milk and cook, stirring constantly, until smooth and thickened. Add the mushrooms and cheese and stir until cheese is melted. Add the eggs, pimento and olives and place in a casserole. Bake at 350 degrees until heated through. Serve over chow mein noodles. 6 servings.

Savory Creamed Mushrooms (above)

165

BAKED PEAS

1 can peas	2 tbsp. milk
1/2 c. tomatoes	2 tbsp. cream
1/2 c. chopped green pepper	Salt to taste
2 tbsp. chopped onion	1 tbsp. melted butter
1/2 tbsp. brown sugar	1/2 c. toasted crumbs

Drain the peas and tomatoes and mix with green pepper and onion. Combine the sugar, milk, cream and salt in a bowl and mix in tomato mixture. Pour into a greased baking dish. Mix the butter and crumbs and sprinkle over tomato mixture. Bake at 325 degrees for 30 minutes. 6 servings.

Mrs. Robert U. Parrot, Alexandria, Louisiana

GREEN PEA CASSEROLE

1 c. chopped onions	1 can pimento strips
1 c. chopped celery	1 can sliced water chestnuts
1 c. chopped green pepper	1 can mushroom soup
1/2 c. butter	1 c. bread crumbs
1 1-lb. can green peas	

Preheat oven to 350 degrees. Cook the onions, celery and green pepper in butter in a saucepan until tender. Add the peas, pimento, water chestnuts and soup and mix well. Place in a casserole and sprinkle bread crumbs on top. Bake for 30 minutes.

Mrs. John C. Wright, Hollywood, Florida

BAKED CHEESE POTATOES

1 tbsp. salad oil	1/4 tsp. pepper
1 clove of garlic, split	1 egg, lightly beaten
4 lge. potatoes, grated	1/4 to 1/2 tsp. nutmeg
2 c. milk	1 c. grated sharp cheese
2 tsp. salt	

Pour oil into a 2-quart baking dish and rub oil around dish with garlic. Combine remaining ingredients and pour into the baking dish. Bake at 325 degrees for 1 hour and 30 minutes. 6 servings.

Mrs. G. L. Robinson, Happy, Texas

CHEESE-POTATO CASSEROLE

4 lge. potatoes	2 slices American process
Salt and pepper to taste	cheese
1/4 c. margarine	1/3 c. evaporated milk

Peel the potatoes and slice thin. Cook in boiling water for about 15 minutes or until almost done, then drain. Place in a 1 1/2-quart casserole and add salt and pepper. Dot with margarine. Cut the cheese in strips and place over potatoes. Pour milk over all and cover casserole. Bake in 400-degree oven for 15 minutes. Uncover and bake for 10 minutes longer or until lightly browned. 4 servings.

Mrs. Cecil S. Mizelle, Greenville, North Carolina

MUSHROOM-SCALLOPED POTATOES

1 can cream of mushroom soup	1/4 c. chopped pimento
2/3 c. evaporated milk	1/2 tsp. salt
3/4 c. grated American cheese	4 c. thinly sliced potatoes

Combine the soup, milk, 1/2 cup cheese, pimento, salt and potatoes and mix well. Place in a greased shallow baking dish and top with remaining cheese. Bake at 350 degrees for 1 hour or until potatoes are tender. 6 servings.

Mrs. Jessie Bard, Depoy, Kentucky

SCALLOPED POTATOES WITH HERBS

4 c. thinly sliced potatoes	1/2 tsp. thyme
Salt and paprika to taste	3 tbsp. butter
1/2 tsp. dried marjoram	1 c. milk
1/2 tsp. savory	1 c. water
1 tsp. chopped parsley	1 c. soft bread crumbs,
1/2 tsp. chopped chives	buttered

Place half the potatoes in a greased baking dish and sprinkle with salt and paprika. Add half the herbs and dot with half the butter. Repeat layers. Pour milk and water over potatoes and cover. Bake at 375 degrees for 40 minutes. Remove cover and sprinkle with bread crumbs. Bake for 15 minutes longer or until brown. 6 servings.

Mrs. Frank Homiller, Ball Ground, Georgia

HERBED SPINACH

1 pkg. frozen chopped spinach	1/3 c. milk
1 c. cooked rice	2 tbsp. chopped onion
1 c. shredded sharp American	1 tsp. Worcestershire sauce
cheese	1 tsp. salt
2 slightly beaten eggs	1/4 tsp. crushed rosemary or
2 tbsp. soft butter or	thyme
margarine	

Cook the spinach according to package directions and drain. Combine all ingredients in a bowl and mix well. Pour into 10 x 6 x 1 1/2-inch baking dish. Bake at 350 degrees for 20 to 25 minutes or until knife inserted in center comes out clean. 6 servings.

Mrs. Edwin McCollom, Henderson, Kentucky

167

Casserole Italiano (below)

CASSEROLE ITALIANO

1 1/2 lb. zucchini	**1 pt. cream-style cottage**
2 tbsp. butter	**cheese**
1 c. minced onion	**1 can tomato soup**
1 sm. clove of garlic, crushed	**2/3 c. water**
1 lb. ground beef	**1 c. shredded sharp American**
1 c. cooked rice	**cheese**
1 tsp. basil	

Cut the zucchini in 1/4-inch slices and cook in a small amount of boiling, salted water in a saucepan until just tender. Drain thoroughly. Melt the butter in a heavy skillet. Add the onion and garlic and cook, stirring, until the onion is transparent. Add the ground beef and cook, stirring occasionally, until beef begins to brown. Stir in the rice and basil. Place half the zucchini in a greased 2 1/2-quart casserole and top with beef mixture. Add the cottage cheese and remaining zucchini. Combine the soup and water and pour over zucchini. Sprinkle with cheese. Bake in 350-degree oven for 35 to 40 minutes or until lightly browned. 6-8 servings.

YELLOW SQUASH CASSEROLE

2 lb. yellow squash	**1 can water chestnuts,**
1 lge. onion	**sliced**
2 tbsp. butter	**Salt to taste**
1 can frozen shrimp soup,	**1 c. bread crumbs**
thawed	

Chop the squash and onion and saute in butter in a saucepan over low heat until tender. Add shrimp soup, water chestnuts and salt and mix well. Pour into a greased casserole. Cover with bread crumbs and dot with additional butter. Bake in a 350-degree oven for 30 minutes. 6-8 servings.

Mrs. John T. Brown, Pine Bluff, Arkansas

BAKED TOMATO AND ZUCCHINI CASSEROLE

3 fresh zucchini
6 sm. onions, sliced
1/3 c. chopped parsley
Salt to taste
1 tsp. dried basil

5 sm. ripe tomatoes,
  sliced
Ground pepper to taste
1/4 c. olive oil

Wash the zucchini and trim both ends. Cook in boiling water for 5 to 10 minutes and drain. Slice 1/2 inch thick and place in a shallow casserole. Add the onions and 1/2 of the parsley and season with salt and basil. Cover with tomatoes and add remaining parsley, pepper and olive oil. Bake at 350 degrees for 30 to 40 minutes or until vegetables are tender. 4 servings.

Mrs. Harvey C. Hamann, Aiken, South Carolina

SAVORY SQUASH

1 lb. summer squash
1/3 c. crumbled saltines
1 onion, chopped
2 tbsp. melted butter
1/2 c. finely diced celery
1/2 c. grated Cheddar cheese

3 tbsp. chopped green chili
  peppers
2 eggs, lightly beaten
1 1/2 c. milk
1 1/4 tsp. salt
Dash of pepper

Cook the squash in boiling water until tender. Drain and mash. Add remaining ingredients and mix well. Pour into a greased baking dish. Bake at 375 degrees for 25 minutes. 6 servings.

Mrs. Lonnie E. Hoeve, Bayrad, New Mexico

CUCUMBERS AU GRATIN

3 tbsp. butter
3 tbsp. flour
1 1/4 c. milk
1 beef bouillon cube
Dash of pepper

1/4 tsp. onion juice
1 c. grated sharp cheese
1/3 c. fine bread crumbs
1 1/2 tbsp. melted butter
2 med. cucumbers

Melt the butter in a saucepan and blend in flour. Add the milk gradually and cook, stirring constantly, until thickened. Stir in bouillon cube, pepper and onion juice and remove from heat. Add the cheese and stir until melted. Mix the bread crumbs and melted butter. Peel the cucumbers and cut in 1/8-inch thick slices. Place alternate layers of cucumbers and cheese sauce in a 6-cup casserole. Top with buttered crumbs and cover. Bake at 325 degrees for about 30 minutes. Remove cover and bake for 10 minutes longer or until brown. Serve hot. 5 servings.

Mrs. M. J. Dutschke, Louisville, Kentucky

169

cereal, pasta, egg, and cheese

These casseroles are a value bonus for today's thrifty southern homemaker. Low in cost, they are high in needed nutritional values. Their hearty flavors are certain to please every family.

Who could resist Cornmeal Souffle, a light-as-air dish featuring one of the all-time favorite southern foods. Another favorite – grits – is the heart of a breakfast-in-a-dish. A Rebel's Deviled Grits combines eggs, bacon, oranges, and grits into a delightfully different casserole.

Rice is still another long-time southern staple. Some of the recipes you will find show it off in extra-special fashion. One, for Rice Pilaf, turns a traditional Mediterranean dish into a typically southern casserole.

Baked Macaroni and Cheese – the family favorite – is featured in several new and different recipes. And don't forget noodles and spaghetti. They take on new flavors in these recipes – as in Noodles Romanoff.

There is also an entire section devoted to favorite southern egg recipes – such as Brunch Eggs, a breakfast casserole so elegant it is right at home on a party table. From Creole country comes Eggs Grinalds, a zesty blend of tomatoes, eggs, and onion.

With so many taste treats awaiting you in this section, your only problem will be deciding which one to try first.

BARLEY CASSEROLE

1/2 lb. fresh mushrooms	1 c. pearl barley
1 lge. onion, chopped	Salt and pepper to taste
4 tbsp. butter	2 to 3 c. boiling beef broth

Slice the mushroom caps and chop stems. Cook the onion in butter in a sauce-pan for 3 to 4 minutes. Add mushrooms and saute for 4 minutes. Add the barley and cook until lightly browned. Add salt and pepper and pour into a greased casserole. Add enough broth to cover mixture by 1/2 inch and cover casserole. Bake at 350 degrees for 25 minutes or until barley is done and liquid absorbed. Chicken broth may be substituted for beef broth. 6 servings.

Mrs. Justin Farley, Richmond, Virginia

CORNMEAL SOUFFLE

3/4 c. cornmeal	1 tbsp. melted fat
2 c. milk	4 eggs, separated
1 tsp. salt	

Cook the cornmeal in milk in a saucepan until thick. Add the salt, fat and beaten egg yolks. Fold in stiffly beaten egg whites and place in a greased casserole. Bake at 350 degrees for 1 hour.

Mrs. Lloyd H. Smith, Easley, South Carolina

A REBEL'S DEVILED GRITS

1 tsp. salt	1 c. orange juice
3 c. boiling water	4 eggs, slightly beaten
1 c. quick-cooking grits	12 slices bacon, partially
1/4 c. butter	cooked
1 tsp. grated orange rind	2 tbsp. brown sugar

Preheat oven to 350 degrees. Add the salt to boiling water in a saucepan and stir in grits slowly. Cook, stirring constantly, for 3 minutes. Remove from heat. Add the butter, orange rind, orange juice and eggs and mix thoroughly. Pour into a greased 1 1/2-quart baking dish. Arrange bacon on top and sprinkle with brown sugar. Bake for 45 minutes or until knife inserted in center comes out clean. 6 servings.

Mavis Thompson, Atlanta, Georgia

FLUFFY GOLDEN GRITS CASSEROLE

2 c. milk	1 tsp. sugar
1/3 c. quick-cooking grits	3 eggs, separated
3/4 tsp. salt	3 tbsp. melted butter

Preheat oven to 375 degrees. Scald the milk in a saucepan. Stir in the grits, salt and sugar and cook for 5 minutes, stirring frequently. Cool. Stir in beaten egg yolks and fold in stiffly beaten egg whites. Pour butter into a baking dish and add grits mixture. Bake for 30 to 40 minutes. Serve hot with additional butter.

Mrs. R. R. Ritter, Falls Church, Virginia

WEST TEXAS-STYLE GRITS

2 c. hot cooked grits	2 cloves of garlic, minced
2 c. grated sharp cheese	2 eggs, well beaten
1/2 c. butter or margarine	1 sm. can green chilies, minced

Mix all ingredients until cheese and butter are melted and place in a casserole. Bake at 300 degrees for 1 hour. 8-10 servings.

Mrs. Donald N. Jones, Tulia, Texas

OATMEAL-PEANUT CASSEROLE

2/3 c. cooked oatmeal	1 c. chopped salted peanuts
1/4 c. chopped green pepper	2/3 c. fine bread crumbs
3 tbsp. minced onion	1/4 lb. cheese, grated
1 tsp. salt	1 egg
2 tsp. lemon juice	1/3 c. milk

Combine all ingredients and mix well. Place in a greased casserole. Bake at 350 degrees for about 1 hour and serve hot with mushroom or tomato sauce. 4 servings.

Mrs. Minnie Pennington, Northport, Alabama

COTTAGE CHEESE AND OATMEAL CASSEROLE

1 c. cottage cheese	1 tbsp. chopped onion
1 c. cold cooked oatmeal	1/2 c. chopped peanuts
1 c. milk	1 lge. can tomatoes
1 egg, slightly beaten	1 sliced onion
1 tbsp. melted butter	8 cloves
Salt and pepper	3 tbsp. butter
1 tsp. poultry seasoning	3 tbsp. flour
Worcestershire sauce to taste	

Mix the cottage cheese and oatmeal in a large mixing bowl. Add the milk and egg and mix well. Add the melted butter, 1/2 teaspoon salt, dash of pepper, poultry seasoning, Worcestershire sauce and chopped onion and mix well. Stir in the peanuts and place in a well-greased casserole. Bake in 350-degree oven until brown. Cook the tomatoes, sliced onion and cloves in a saucepan for 20 minutes. Brown the butter in a frying pan and stir in flour. Cook until smooth and brown, stirring constantly, and add salt and pepper to taste. Add the tomato mixture and heat through. Serve with oatmeal mixture.

Mrs. Grace Hutzler, Houston, Texas

University Casserole (below)

UNIVERSITY CASSEROLE

1/4 c. butter	1 c. shredded American
3 tbsp. flour	process cheese
1 1/4 tsp. salt	3 c. cooked rice
2 c. milk	6 slices cooked bacon, crumbled
2 tsp. prepared mustard	6 tomato slices

Melt 3 tablespoons butter in a saucepan and blend in flour and 1 teaspoon salt. Add the milk and cook, stirring constantly, until smooth and thickened. Add the mustard and cheese and stir until cheese is melted. Stir in the rice and bacon and pour into a greased 1 1/2-quart shallow casserole. Bake at 375 degrees for about 20 minutes or until heated through. Arrange tomato slices on rice mixture. Dot with remaining butter and sprinkle with remaining salt. Bake for 5 minutes longer. 6 servings.

ARROZ CON JOCOQUE

3/4 lb. Jack cheese	3 c. cooked rice
3 c. sour cream	Salt and pepper to taste
2 c. diced green chilies	1/2 c. grated Cheddar cheese

Cut the Jack cheese in strips. Mix the sour cream and green chilies. Place half the rice in a greased casserole and add salt and pepper. Add the sour cream mixture, then add cheese strips. Add remaining rice. Bake at 350 degrees for 30 minutes. Sprinkle Cheddar cheese on top and bake until cheese is melted. 8 servings.

Mrs. Francis Rodolphe Milton, Wetumpka, Alabama

ARKANSAS COUNTY RICE

4 c. cooked rice
2 1-lb. cans tomatoes
1 bell pepper, diced

Salt and pepper to taste
1 1/2 c. grated cheese

Mix the rice, tomatoes, bell pepper, salt and pepper and place in a casserole. Cover with cheese. Bake at 350 degrees for 20 minutes or until cheese is melted. 8 servings.

Mrs. E. D. Eldridge, Almyra, Arkansas

BROWN RICE CASSEROLE

1/2 c. margarine
1 c. long grain rice

1 can onion soup
1 can beef consomme

Melt the margarine in a casserole and stir in the rice, soup and consomme. Bake at 325 degrees for 1 hour.

Mrs. Rebecca K. Ford, Chester, South Carolina

CHINESE-FRIED RICE

2 tbsp. oil
2 lge. onions, chopped
2 c. cooked rice
1 to 2 tbsp. soy sauce

1/2 tsp. salt
2 c. chopped cooked meat (opt.)
2 tbsp. diced carrots
2 tbsp. green peas

Heat the oil in a saucepan and cook onions in oil until tender. Add the rice, soy sauce and salt and mix well. Stir in the meat and place in a casserole. Add carrots and peas. Bake at 350 degrees until heated through. Serve hot. 6 servings.

Mrs. Collis H. Ivery, Barksdale, Louisiana

EPICUREAN WILD RICE

1/3 c. butter or margarine
1/2 c. snipped parsley
1/2 c. chopped green onions
1 c. diagonally sliced celery
1 1/4 c. wild rice

1 can consomme
1 1/2 c. boiling water
1 tsp. salt
1/2 tsp. dried marjoram
1/2 c. sherry

Melt the butter in a Dutch oven and add parsley, onions and celery. Saute until soft but not browned. Add rice, consomme, water, salt and marjoram and cover. Bake at 350 degrees for about 45 minutes, stirring occasionally and adding hot water, if needed. Remove cover and stir in the sherry. Bake for about 5 minutes longer or until sherry is absorbed. 6 servings.

Mrs. Dan P. Johnston, Dallas, Texas

EXOTIC RICE CASSEROLE

2 c. rice	1/2 c. butter
2 cans beef consomme	1 5-oz. can water chestnuts
2 lge. onions, chopped	1 4 1/2-oz. can sliced
1 c. chopped celery	mushrooms

Cook the rice according to package directions, substituting consomme for water. Saute the onions and celery in butter in a saucepan until soft and light brown. Slice the water chestnuts and add to onion mixture. Add the mushrooms and simmer for 10 to 15 minutes. Place alternate layers of rice and onion mixture in a 10 x 14-inch casserole and cover casserole with foil. Bake in a 300-degree oven for 30 minutes. 10-12 servings.

Mrs. Mayme McLean, Liberty, Texas

PARTY GREEN RICE

2 c. rice	1/2 lb. mild Cheddar cheese,
1 1/2 to 2 c. milk	grated
1/2 c. salad oil	1/2 lb. sharp Cheddar cheese,
1/4 c. chopped parsley	grated
1 c. chopped green peppers	Salt and pepper to taste
1 c. chopped green onions and	2 garlic cloves, minced
tops	

Cook the rice according to package directions. Add remaining ingredients and mix well. Pour into a casserole and cover. Bake at 350 degrees for 1 hour.

Mrs. Alice Griffin, Mt. Enterprise, Texas

RICE AND CHEESE CASSEROLE

6 slices bacon	1/2 tsp. salt
1 c. minced onion	1 tsp. thyme
1 c. diced celery	1/2 tsp. pepper
3 c. cooked rice	1 can cream of chicken soup
1 c. sliced stuffed olives	2 c. grated Cheddar cheese

Fry the bacon in a large skillet until crisp and remove from skillet. Drain well on absorbent paper and crumble. Drain all but 3 tablespoons drippings from skillet. Add the onion and celery to skillet and cook until tender. Remove from heat and stir in the rice, olives and seasonings. Heat the soup and 1 cup cheese in a saucepan until cheese is melted and add to rice mixture. Add the bacon and mix. Turn into a greased casserole and top with remaining cheese. Bake at 375 degrees for about 15 minutes or until browned. One can chicken broth may be substituted for chicken soup. 6-8 servings.

Mrs. Jane S. Howard, Stuttgart, Arkansas

GREEN RICE CASSEROLE

1 1/2 c. cooked rice	3/4 c. chopped parsley
3/4 c. grated sharp cheese	1/2 c. milk or consomme (opt.)
3 tbsp. melted butter	1/2 tsp. salt
1 1/2 tbsp. chopped onion	2 eggs, separated

Combine the rice, cheese, butter, onion, parsley, milk and salt in a mixing bowl. Add the well-beaten egg yolks and mix well. Fold in stiffly beaten egg whites and place in a 1-quart casserole. Bake at 350 degrees for 25 minutes and serve immediately. 4 servings.

Mrs. Raymond White, Savannah, Georgia

HAWAIIAN RICE

1 c. rice	1 c. water
1 can bouillon or consomme	1 sm. can green chilies,
1/2 c. melted margarine	chopped

Mix all ingredients in a casserole. Bake at 350 degrees for 1 hour.

Mrs. Paul Wecker, Midland, Texas

JALAPENO RICE CASSEROLE

3/4 c. rice	1 lb. mild Monterey cheese,
2 c. sour cream	grated
1 tsp. salt	Butter
1 6-oz. can green chilies	

Prepare rice according to package directions and stir in the sour cream and salt. Chop the green chilies. Place alternate layers of rice mixture, green chilies and cheese in a casserole and dot with butter. Bake at 350 degrees for 30 minutes.

Mrs. Roy A. Smith, Arlington, Virginia

RICE PILAF

1 can beef consomme	2/3 c. chopped celery
1 consomme can water	2/3 c. chopped green onion tops
1/2 c. margarine	2/3 c. chopped blanched almonds
2 c. long grain rice	1 tsp. monosodium glutamate
2/3 c. chopped carrots	1 tsp. chopped parsley

Preheat oven to 325 degrees. Heat a 2-quart baking dish in oven. Pour the consomme and water into a saucepan and bring to a boil. Melt the margarine in a saucepan and add rice. Cook, stirring constantly, for 2 to 3 minutes or until rice is hot. Pour consomme mixture and rice into the hot baking dish and cover. Bake for 45 minutes. Add remaining ingredients and mix well. Cover and bake for 10 minutes longer or until vegetables are tender.

Mrs. T. L. Graham, Eclectic, Alabama

APPLE-MACARONI AND CHEESE

1/2 lb. sliced bacon	1/4 lb. shredded cheese
1 onion, diced	1/4 tsp. curry powder
1/2 lb. elbow macaroni	1/8 tsp. dry mustard
1 8-oz. can tomato sauce	1/2 tsp. Worcestershire sauce
2 c. applesauce	Salt and pepper to taste

Fry the bacon in a skillet until crisp and drain on paper towels. Reserve 4 slices for garnish and crumble remaining slices. Drain off all but 2 tablespoons bacon fat from skillet and saute onion in bacon fat until tender. Cook the macaroni according to package directions. Add the onion, crumbled bacon and remaining ingredients and mix well. Place in a 2-quart casserole. Bake at 350 degrees for 20 minutes. Place reserved bacon slices on top and bake for 5 minutes longer. 4-6 servings.

Mrs. J. Q. Beasley, Tallahassee, Florida

CHEESE-A-RONI WITH MUSHROOM SAUCE

1 1/3 c. elbow macaroni	1/2 tsp. salt
3 eggs, separated	Pepper to taste
1 c. warm milk	1 c. grated American cheese
2 tbsp. melted butter	2/3 c. soft bread crumbs
3 tbsp. minced parsley	1 can cream of mushroom soup
3 tbsp. chopped stuffed olives	1/2 soup can milk
2 tsp. minced onion	

Cook the macaroni according to package directions. Rinse and drain. Beat the egg yolks until light and add milk gradually. Add the butter and mix well. Add parsley, olives, onion, salt and pepper and mix well. Add the cheese, bread crumbs and macaroni and fold in stiffly beaten egg whites. Spoon into a well-greased 9 x 5 x 3-inch loaf pan. Bake at 325 degrees for 1 hour. Mix the soup and milk in a saucepan and place over medium heat until heated through, stirring frequently. Serve with macaroni mixture. 6 servings.

Mrs. Hugh Paton, Knoxville, Tennessee

BAKED MACARONI AND CHEESE

1 c. cooked macaroni	2 eggs
2 slices bread, crumbled	1 tsp. chopped green pepper
1 tsp. chopped onion	1 tbsp. butter
1 c. grated cheese	Salt and pepper to taste
1 1/2 c. milk	Paprika to taste

Combine all ingredients and mix well. Place in a well-greased baking dish. Bake in 350-degree oven for 40 minutes. 6 servings.

Elaine Fish, Joseph City, Arizona

GREEN PEPPER-CHEESE CASSEROLE

3 c. water
1 tsp. salt
1 c. elbow macaroni
1 green pepper, sliced

1 c. grated cheese
8 saltine crackers, crumbled
3/4 c. milk

Pour the water into a saucepan and bring to boiling point. Add the salt and macaroni and cook for about 15 minutes. Drain. Cook the green pepper in boiling water for 5 minutes and drain. Place alternate layers of macaroni, green pepper, cheese and cracker crumbs in a casserole and pour milk over top. Bake at 375 degrees for 30 to 35 minutes. 6 servings.

Mrs. Willis E. Wise, Pineville, Kentucky

GARDEN PATCH MACARONI CASSEROLE

1 7-oz. package elbow
  macaroni
2 qt. coarsely shredded
  cabbage
3/4 c. cooked carrot slices
3/4 c. cooked peas

1 tsp. seasoned salt
1 tbsp. chopped chives
1 can cream of mushroom soup
2 c. sour cream
1 1/2 tsp. salt
1 c. shredded American cheese

Cook the macaroni in boiling, salted water until just tender and drain. Cook the cabbage in boiling, salted water for 6 to 7 minutes or until tender-crisp and drain. Add the macaroni, carrot slices, peas, seasoned salt and chives. Mix the soup and sour cream and fold into macaroni mixture. Add the salt and mix well. Place in a greased 2 1/2-quart baking dish and sprinkle with cheese. Bake at 350 degrees for 25 to 30 minutes or until heated through and cheese is melted. 8-10 servings.

Garden Patch Macaroni Casserole (above)

Tomato-Cheese Casserole (below)

TOMATO-CHEESE CASSEROLE

1 7-oz. package elbow macaroni	1/8 tsp. pepper
6 slices bacon	2 c. milk
3 tbsp. butter	2 c. shredded sharp American
3 tbsp. flour	cheese
1 1/2 tsp. salt	3 med. tomatoes, sliced
	Paprika (opt.)

Cook the macaroni in 2 quarts boiling, salted water until tender and drain. Fry the bacon in a skillet until crisp and drain. Cool and crumble. Melt tne butter in a saucepan over low heat and blend in the flour, salt and pepper. Add the milk and cook, stirring constantly, until smooth and thickened. Remove from heat. Add 1 1/2 cups cheese and stir until cheese is melted. Add the bacon and mix well. Place half the macaroni in a greased 2-quart baking dish. Reserve 4 tomato slices. Arrange half the remaining tomato slices on macaroni and cover with half the cheese sauce. Repeat layers. Garnish with reserved tomato slices and sprinkle with remaining cheese. Sprinkle with paprika. Bake in 350-degree oven for about 30 minutes or until brown. 8 servings.

BAKED MACARONI AND TOMATOES AU GRATIN

4 tbsp. melted butter or margarine	Dash of cayenne
2 tbsp. dry bread crumbs	2 15-oz. cans macaroni with cheese sauce
1/4 c. chopped onion	3 hard-cooked eggs, sliced
1/4 c. sour cream	1 lge. tomato, sliced
1/2 tsp. salt	Parsley sprigs

Preheat oven to 350 degrees. Mix 2 tablespoons butter with bread crumbs and set aside. Saute the onion in remaining butter in a small skillet for about 3 minutes or until golden. Remove from heat. Add the sour cream, salt and cayenne and mix well. Place 1 can macaroni into a 1 1/2-quart casserole and place 2 eggs over macaroni. Add sour cream mixture, then remaining macaroni. Arrange tomato slices around edge and sprinkle with buttered crumbs. Bake for 30 to 35 minutes or until hot and bubbly and garnish with remaining egg and parsley. 6 servings.

Mrs. G. L. Shoemake, Yazoo City, Mississippi

MACARONI AND CHEESE SAUCE

Salt	1/4 tsp. dry mustard (opt.)
2 c. elbow macaroni	1/8 tsp. pepper
4 tbsp. butter or margarine	2 c. milk
1 sm. onion, minced	2 c. grated Cheddar cheese
1 tbsp. flour	3/4 c. bread crumbs

Preheat oven to 400 degrees. Pour 3 quarts water into a saucepan and add 1 tablespoon salt. Bring to boiling point and add macaroni slowly. Cook for 9 minutes, stirring frequently, then drain. Place in a casserole. Melt 2 tablespoons butter in a double boiler and add onion. Stir in the flour, mustard, 3/4 teaspoon salt and pepper. Stir in milk slowly and cook until smooth and hot, stirring frequently. Add 1 1/4 cups cheese and stir until cheese is melted. Pour over macaroni and toss lightly. Top with remaining cheese. Toss bread crumbs with remaining melted butter and sprinkle over cheese. Bake for 20 minutes. 4-6 servings.

Carolyn Rose Nash, Baxter, Tennessee

COTTAGE NOODLE CASSEROLE

Salt	2 c. milk
3 qt. boiling water	2 c. cream-style cottage cheese
8 oz. wide egg noodles	1 1-lb. can applesauce
1 env. cream of leek soup mix	1/4 c. raisins
1/4 c. butter or margarine	1 c. grated sharp Cheddar cheese
1/4 tsp. pepper	
1/4 tsp. dry mustard	

Add 1 tablespoon salt to boiling water and add noodles gradually so that water continues to boil. Cook, stirring occasionally, until tender and drain in a colander. Combine the soup mix, butter, 1/4 teaspoon salt, pepper, mustard and milk in a saucepan. Cook over medium heat, stirring constantly, until thickened. Add the noodles, cottage cheese, applesauce, raisins and 1/2 cup cheese and mix well. Turn into a 2 1/2-quart baking dish and sprinkle with remaining cheese. Bake in 350-degree oven for about 30 minutes or until bubbly.

Photograph for this recipe on page 170.

POLISH PASTA

1/4 c. butter or margarine	1 carton cottage cheese
1/4 c. flour	2 tsp. chopped parsley
2 1/2 c. milk	1 tsp. oregano
1/2 c. sour cream	Salt and pepper to taste
2 eggs, lightly beaten	1 pkg. sliced mozzarella cheese
1 12-oz. package elbow	1/4 c. grated Italian cheese
macaroni	1/4 c. bread crumbs

Melt the butter in a saucepan and blend in the flour. Add milk gradually. Add the sour cream and 1 egg and cook over medium heat until thick, stirring constantly. Cook the macaroni according to package directions and drain. Add the sour cream mixture and mix well. Combine the cottage cheese, parsley, remaining egg, oregano, salt and pepper and mix well. Place half the macaroni mixture in a greased 2-quart casserole. Cover with cottage cheese mixture and add mozzarella cheese. Add remaining macaroni mixture. Combine Italian cheese and bread crumbs and sprinkle over macaroni mixture. Bake in 350-degree oven for 30 to 40 minutes. 6 servings.

Mrs. Franklin Barker, Glen Burnie, Maryland

GREEN NOODLES CASSEROLE

3 c. green noodles	2 1/2 c. milk
3/4 tsp. hot sauce	1 c. diced sharp Cheddar cheese
1/4 c. butter	1/4 c. grated Parmesan cheese
1/4 c. flour	1 4-oz. can pimento, diced
1 tsp. salt	3 hard-cooked eggs, sliced

Cook the noodles according to package directions, adding 1/4 teaspoon hot sauce to water. Drain and rinse. Melt the butter in a saucepan and stir in flour, salt and remaining hot sauce. Add the milk and stir over medium heat until smooth and slightly thickened. Add the cheeses and stir until melted. Add the pimento and noodles and mix. Pour into a 1 1/2-quart casserole. Bake at 350 degrees for about 25 minutes. Top with eggs and bake for 5 minutes longer. 6-8 servings.

Anna Kate Eatman, Tuscaloosa, Alabama

NOODLE LAYER PUDDING

1 lb. cottage cheese, drained	1 tsp. salt
4 egg yolks	1 lb. broad noodles
1/2 c. heavy cream	1/4 c. bread crumbs
2 tbsp. sugar	4 tbsp. melted butter

Mix the cottage cheese with egg yolks, cream, sugar and salt in a bowl until smooth. Cook the noodles according to package directions and drain. Layer the noodles and cottage cheese mixture in a greased baking dish, beginning and ending with noodles. Mix the bread crumbs and butter and sprinkle over noodles. Bake at 375 degrees for 30 minutes. 4-6 servings.

Mrs. Everett A. Towns, Dallas, Texas

NOODLES ROMANOFF

2 8-oz. packages egg noodles	1 bunch green onions, finely
3 c. large-curd cottage cheese	chopped
2 tsp. Worcestershire sauce	1/2 tsp. hot sauce
2 cloves of garlic, mashed	1 c. grated Parmesan cheese
1 pt. thick sour cream	

Cook the noodles according to package directions. Add remaining ingredients except Parmesan cheese and mix well. Pour into a greased casserole and sprinkle with Parmesan cheese. Bake at 350 degrees for 25 minutes. 16-18 servings.

Anna P. Williams, Hobbs, New Mexico

WATERCRESS-NOODLE CASSEROLE

1/4 c. margarine	2 tbsp. wine vinegar
2 tbsp. finely chopped onion	1/2 c. shredded Parmesan cheese
3 tbsp. flour	1/2 c. sliced ripe olives
1/2 tsp. salt	1 c. snipped watercress
1/4 tsp. white pepper	8 oz. wide noodles
2 c. cream	Buttered bread crumbs

Melt the margarine in a saucepan. Add the onion and cook for about 3 minutes or until soft. Blend in flour, salt and pepper and heat until bubbling, stirring constantly. Remove from heat and add cream gradually, blending well. Return to heat and bring to a boil. Cook for 1 to 2 minutes longer. Remove from heat and stir in vinegar. Add the cheese and stir until melted. Stir in the olives and watercress. Cook the noodles according to package directions and drain. Add the olive mixture and mix. Turn into a casserole and cover with buttered bread crumbs. Bake in 350-degree oven until brown. 8-10 servings.

Mrs. Laura Gwyer, Autaugaville, Alabama

CHEESE AND SPAGHETTI CASSEROLE

2 c. broken spaghetti	1 1/2 tbsp. chopped pimento
1 1/2 c. milk	1 c. corn flake crumbs
1/4 c. margarine	1 1/2 c. grated cheese

Cook the spaghetti in boiling, salted water until tender and drain. Add the milk, margarine, pimento and corn flake crumbs and mix well. Turn into a greased casserole and top with cheese. Bake at 350 degrees for about 30 minutes.

Mrs. Ethel M. Alston, Littleton, North Carolina

SPAGHETTI-CHEESE BAKE

1 1/2 boxes spaghetti
2 c. cottage cheese
1 can tomato sauce

1 can pimentos, chopped
1 sm. can evaporated milk
1 tsp. salt

Cook the spaghetti according to package directions. Add remaining ingredients and mix well. Pour into a casserole. Bake at 325 degrees until brown. 4-6 servings.

Phyllistine Wilson, Banks, Arkansas

BRUNCH EGGS

3 doz. eggs
1/4 c. milk
2 cans cream of mushroom soup
1/2 c. sherry

1 lge. can mushrooms, drained
1/4 lb. butter
1/2 lb. Cheddar cheese, grated
Paprika

Beat the eggs in a bowl and stir in the milk. Heat the soup in a saucepan and stir until smooth. Add sherry and mushrooms. Scramble the egg mixture in butter in a skillet until just soft. Place half the eggs in a casserole and add half the soup mixture. Add half the cheese and repeat layers. Sprinkle with paprika. Bake at 300 degrees for about 1 hour.

Mrs. R. H. Carter, Wetumpka, Alabama

EGG SALAD CASSEROLE

8 hard-cooked eggs, chopped
1 1/2 c. diced celery
1 tsp. minced onion
1/2 tsp. salt

2/3 c. mayonnaise
1 c. grated sharp American
cheese
1 c. crushed potato chips

Combine all ingredients except cheese and potato chips and toss lightly. Turn into 4 individual casseroles and sprinkle with cheese and potato chips. Bake at 375 degrees for 25 minutes. 4 servings.

Debra Bailey, Lutts, Tennessee

EGGS BECHAMEL

6 hard-boiled eggs
4 onions
4 tbsp. butter

1 1/2 c. hot Bechamel Sauce
Salt to taste
Freshly ground pepper to taste

Slice the eggs and place in a casserole. Slice the onions and saute in butter in a saucepan until soft. Add the Bechamel Sauce, salt and pepper and mix well. Pour over the eggs. Bake in 350-degree oven until heated through.

Bechamel Sauce

1/2 c. butter
1/2 onion, finely chopped

6 tbsp. flour
4 c. hot milk

2 oz. lean veal or ham,	**1/2 bay leaf**
chopped	**White peppercorns to taste**
1 stalk celery, finely chopped	**Freshly grated nutmeg to taste**
1 sm. sprig of thyme	

Melt 6 tablespoons butter in top of a double boiler. Add the onion and cook over low heat until transparent. Stir in the flour. Add the milk and cook, stirring constantly, until thick and smooth. Place the veal and celery in remaining butter in a saucepan over low heat. Season with thyme, bay leaf, peppercorns and nutmeg and cook for 5 minutes, stirring constantly. Add to the white sauce and place over hot water. Cook for 45 minutes to 1 hour, stirring occasionally. Strain through a fine sieve into a bowl, pressing veal and onion well to extract all liquid. Cover surface with small pieces of additional butter to keep film from forming.

Mrs. W. D. Smith, Wetumpka, Alabama

CRUNCHY BAKED EGGS AU GRATIN

3 tbsp. shortening	**2 tsp. angostura aromatic**
1/4 c. flour	**bitters**
1/8 tsp. paprika	**1/2 c. grated American**
1 tsp. salt	**cheese**
2 c. milk	**3 c. toasted bread cubes**
2 tbsp. chopped green pepper	**6 hard-cooked eggs, halved**

Preheat oven to 350 degrees. Melt the shortening in a saucepan and stir in the flour, paprika and salt. Stir in milk gradually and cook over low heat, stirring constantly, until smooth and thick. Add the green pepper, angostura bitters and cheese and stir until cheese is melted. Fold in 2 cups bread cubes. Arrange eggs in a well-greased 1 1/2-quart casserole and pour cheese sauce over eggs. Top with remaining bread cubes. Bake for 20 minutes or until lightly browned. 6 servings.

Crunchy Baked Eggs Au Gratin (above)

Baked Omelet (below)

BAKED OMELET

6 eggs, separated	**1/3 c. water**
1/4 c. cornstarch	**1 tsp. salt**

Beat the egg whites in a large bowl until stiff but not dry. Beat the egg yolks with cornstarch, water and salt until light and fold into egg whites. Pour into a greased baking dish. Bake in a 350-degree oven for about 15 minutes or until dry on top. Serve immediately. 6 servings.

CREOLE EGGS GRINALDS

1 med. onion, chopped fine	**3 tbsp. flour**
2 tbsp. bacon fat	**1 c. milk**
1 lge. can tomatoes	**8 hard-boiled eggs, sliced**
Salt and pepper to taste	**1 c. toasted bread crumbs**
1/2 c. butter	

Brown the onion in hot bacon fat in a saucepan. Add the tomatoes and simmer until onion is tender. Add the salt and pepper. Melt 1/4 cup butter in a saucepan and stir in the flour. Add the milk and cook, stirring, until thick. Add tomato mixture and stir well. Place alternate layers of tomato mixture, eggs and bread crumbs in a greased casserole and dot with remaining butter. Bake in 400-degree oven for 25 minutes.

Mrs. G. C. Booker, Theodore, Alabama

EGG AND MUSHROOM CASSEROLE

1 doz. hard-boiled eggs	**1/2 tsp. pepper**
1/2 c. mayonnaise	**1 med. can sliced mushrooms**
1 tbsp. mustard	**Rich cream sauce**
1 tsp. Worcestershire sauce	**1 c. grated sharp cheese**
1 tsp. salt	**3/4 c. cracker crumbs**

Halve the eggs lengthwise and remove yolks. Mash egg yolks and mix with mayonnaise, mustard, Worcestershire sauce, salt, pepper and mushrooms. Stuff egg whites and arrange in layers in a casserole, covering each layer with cream sauce. Mix the cheese and cracker crumbs and sprinkle on top. Bake at 350 degrees until cheese in melted and lightly browned. 10-12 servings.

Mrs. Myrtle Trice Sands, Waycross, Georgia

ITALIAN CHEESE SOUFFLE

1/3 c. finely chopped onion
1/4 c. butter or margarine
1/4 c. flour
1 tbsp. dry mustard
1/2 tsp. salt
1/2 tsp. paprika
1 c. milk
5 egg yolks, beaten

1   8-oz. package pasteurized
    process cheese spread
1   8-oz. can tomato sauce
1/4 tsp. oregano leaves
1 1/2 c. finely crushed
    saltine crackers
6 egg whites

Saute the onion in butter in a saucepan for about 5 minutes and blend in the flour, mustard, salt and paprika. Add milk gradually and bring to a boil over medium heat, stirring constantly. Remove from heat. Blend a small amount of hot mixture into egg yolks, then stir back into saucepan. Add the cheese, tomato sauce and oregano and stir until cheese is melted. Cool, then stir in cracker crumbs. Beat egg whites until stiff and fold into cheese mixture. Pour into an ungreased 2-quart casserole. Bake at 350 degrees for 30 to 40 minutes. Place tent of foil over casserole and bake for 20 minutes longer. Serve at once. 6 servings.

Italian Cheese Souffle (above)

CHEESE AND EGG CASSEROLE

10 slices bread	1 tsp. salt
Butter	Dash of pepper
1/2 lb. New York State cheese, grated	6 eggs, beaten
3 c. milk	Paprika

Remove crusts from bread. Butter bread well and cut into cubes. Place half the cubes in a greased shallow baking dish and add half the cheese. Repeat layers. Mix the milk, salt, pepper and eggs and pour over cheese. Refrigerate for several hours or overnight. Sprinkle with paprika and place in pan of water. Bake at 300 degrees for 1 hour and 30 minutes. 8 servings.

Mrs. Eleanor L. Miller, Mason, West Virginia

CHEESE PUDDING

1 c. crumbled crackers	1 4-oz. can pimentos, chopped
1/4 lb. American cheese, grated	Milk
4 hard-cooked eggs, sliced	

Place alternate layers of cracker crumbs, cheese, eggs and pimentos in a baking dish and add enough milk to come to top layer of cheese. Bake at 350 degrees until light brown. 6-8 servings.

Mrs. Elmer Rogers, Hodgenville, Kentucky

PRESIDENT'S CHEESE PUDDING

1 c. cracker crumbs	1 7-oz. can pimento, chopped
2 c. medium white sauce	4 hard-cooked eggs, grated
1/2 lb. American cheese, grated	Buttered crumbs

Place alternate layers of cracker crumbs, white sauce, cheese, pimento and eggs in a greased baking dish and cover with buttered crumbs. Bake at 350 degrees for 25 minutes. 8 servings.

Ella Rose Allen, Bardstown, Kentucky

CHILI VERDE CON QUESO

4 tortillas	1 lb. longhorn cheese, shredded
1 lge. can green chilies, chopped	2 4-oz. cans tomato sauce
	1/2 2-oz. can hot sauce

Place 1 tortilla in a greased large casserole. Cover with 1/4 of the green chilies and 1/4 of the cheese. Mix tomato sauce with hot sauce and place 1/4 of the mixture over cheese. Repeat layers until all ingredients are used. Bake at 300 degrees until bubbly. Cut in 6 wedges and serve with shredded lettuce. 6 servings.

Doris C. Dunford, Flagstaff, Arizona

INDEX

PHOTOGRAPHY CREDITS: International Tuna Fish Association; National Macaroni Institute; National Kraut Packers Association; Spanish Green Olive Commission; Brussels Sprouts Marketing Program; California Artichoke Advisory Board; Louisiana Yam Commission; United Fresh Fruit and Vegetable Association; National Broiler Council; Tuna Research Foundation; McIlhenny Company; National Livestock and Meat Board; American Home Foods: Chef-Boy-Ar-Dee; Florida Fresh Fruit and Vegetable Association; American Mushroom Institute; Campbell Soup Company; Canned Salmon Institute; Best Foods: Division of Corn Products Company International, Incorporated; Procter and Gamble Company: Crisco Division; Grandma's West Indies Molasses; Florida Citrus Commission; National Dairy Council; American Dairy Association; Quaker Oats Company; California Beef Council; The Aluminum Association; Processed Apples Institute; California Prune Advisory Board; Olive Administrative Committee; Evaporated Milk Association; American Lamb Council; American Dry Milk Institute; Angostura-Wuppermann Corporation; National Biscuit Company.

Printed in the United States of America.